A SURVIVOR'S STORY

Second Edition

ISBN-13: 978-0-9833310-7-0
ISBN-10: 0983331073

Paperback ISBN: 978-0-9833310-3-2

LCCN: 2011920355

Published by Aperture Press, LLC
Reading, PA
www.AperturePress.net

First Printing 1999

A SURVIVOR'S STORY

The Personal Memoirs
of Severin Fayerman

The Author - Severin Fayerman

Contents

Dedication

I wish to dedicate this work to John Moore, a fine man who followed my writing as it evolved but passed away before I completed my Memoirs. Every time his wife Louise gave him the latest segment of my work to read and review, he couldn't wait until the next section was written. I often muse how happy he would have been upon reading the completed text in which he had such a deep and sincere interest.

I also want to thank Louise Moore, my former secretary, for laboriously editing these Memoirs. Her remarks, constructive criticism, and infinite patience made it possible for my work to emerge in its present form.

Boonecroft Farms 1999

Preface

Throughout the years I have been pressed by family and friends to write about my life during World War II, coming to America, and the founding of Baldwin Hardware Mfg. Corp. However, every time I considered doing so I decided against it because I did not want to revive in my memory the horrible events of the concentration camps, which I had tried so very hard to forget.

In recent years, though, I have been asked to tell my story to various groups and organizations. After repeating the speech a number of times and realizing what a strong impact A Survivor's Story had on my audience, I came to the conclusion that I had an obligation to write my memoirs. I do so now so that present and future generations will not forget the horrors of war, and to honor the countless number of innocent victims who did not survive. Also, I welcomed the opportunity to express my love and respect for this country. Where but in America could a penniless immigrant, endowed only with the desire to succeed, realize success beyond his wildest dreams? I remember the unbelievable opportunity my family saw and seized upon and the hard and tedious work, which, with the help of my wife Marjorie, allowed us to literally build a company from scratch - one which has become a household name in our country and abroad. I believe this can still be accomplished today. Hopefully, my story will give encouragement to other enterprising individuals who want to follow in my footsteps and pursue the American dream.

The Beginning

I was born on March 18, 1922, in Bendzin, Poland, the only child of Felicia and Henry Fayerman. The town was located near the border of Germany. I led a very protected life as a member of a middle class family. Fortunately, my parents appreciated the value of a good education. They were very displeased with my academic achievements and I, therefore, had tutors most of my school years. I managed, however, to learn to speak both German and French while I was in elementary school. Later, I was enrolled in a local, private school. My school marks didn't improve, and I failed again, having to repeat one academic year.

In the year 1932, my father became a partner in a woolen plant in Bielsko and we all moved to that lovely, industrial textile mill town located at the foot of the picturesque Beskidy Mountains. We lived, as is customary in Europe, in an apartment building on the outskirts of town. We had a full view of mountains from most windows. I reached my teens there and partook in many winter sports, especially skiing. My school work improved slightly as I was now enrolled in a public high school for boys. These were most probably my happiest years, a period I remember fondly.

My father in the year 1935 sold his interest in the woolen company named Triangle in the Circle, which, by the way, still exists to this day. He took a job as director of a crystal manufacturing plant near Warsaw. My mother and I stayed behind for about a year. It was only a temporary job for him as he, his father John, and other family members began organizing a new manufacturing facility in Bendzin.

The following year we moved to Katowice, a large city in Upper Silesia, several miles from Bendzin. My father left the job near Warsaw and joined the

1

already organized company which he named "Silesia." The move coincided with my increased interest in learning and I advanced to the head of my class. I took English as my foreign modern language and seriously applied myself to school work.

On September 1, 1939, the war broke out with Germany. The Germans crossed the border only about twenty-five miles from Katowice. I was about to begin the last year of high school. Instead, I volunteered in the Polish army. My parents left the city to join the rest of the family in Bendzin and to be near the "Silesia" factory. However, with the outbreak of the war, the employees did not show up for work and the factory was closed.

As a volunteer, I walked for about three days in search of the retreating army. When I finally joined the nearest outfit we were told by our commanding officer to lay down our arms and surrender to the advancing German army. It was simply a matter of German tanks catching up with the slow marching Polish army. The Polish resistance was shattered within the first week of the war. Only the capital of Warsaw resisted and was devastated by the superior German war machine.

I limped back home to find the whole family busily at work in the plant. My father decided to reopen the factory to occupy everyone who wanted to forget what was happening around them. Amazingly, the business restarted very quickly. This was due to the fact that Germany simply annexed Silesia into the Reich. Thus, we became German subjects encouraged to resume our normal lives.

The following spring the government began to tighten control over the industry. Poles no longer were allowed to own and operate manufacturing facilities. We had to get a German supervisor who would direct the company. Thus, we became employees in our own business. Fortunately, father had a friend who agreed to take the position of supervisor in title only. We were able to run the company as our own. My father spoke perfect German and when the government inspectors came he impersonated the supervisor.

1940 and 1941 were "golden years" for our business in that we made a lot of money and converted cash to gold objects, which we hid. Unfortunately, the events around us began to deteriorate with each month. There were constant police actions. Units of the military and police would block off sections of the town, stop every able looking person and ask for documents. If one was not employed in a vital industry, it meant deportation to work camps in Germany.

Fortunately, our plant had the status of "war importance." People employed in our plant were safe for the time being. But events were turning from bad to worse. German cities were bombed and the refugees came to our town dispossessing Polish citizens. My parents and I had to give up a beautiful, fully furnished apartment and were allowed to take only our personal belongings with us. We moved into an old house near the plant with the rest of father's family.

At the beginning of 1942 the attention of the Germans was turning toward the Polish Jewish population. Our Jewish employees lost the status of being important to the war effort and were summarily sent to work camps in Germany. During the police actions many would hide in the factory to avoid deportation, at least until the next razzia (police raid).

This was also a very bad year for our family personally. Our benefactor, the German supervisor, died suddenly. We were distraught, but fortunately, (so we thought at the time) a close cousin of our former supervisor agreed to take his place. This time, however, we were not so lucky. Mr. P (as we shall call him) insisted on actually managing the company. My father remained as his assistant but lost his previous influence. Also, this same year my grandfather John lost his life in an industrial accident in our plant.

The dark clouds began to gather over us. Mr. P. however could be bribed. We managed to carry on the business and still make a lot of money. Mr. P. brought two important diversifications to our screw and hardware business. We undertook repairs of sewing machines for several large military clothing manufacturers and also made small aircraft parts. Later, we added an important department of electrical gear overhaul for aircraft engines. Now we were really engaged in industry important to the war effort. We were secure for the time being.

The year 1943 brought increased pressure on the Jewish community. The Germans were summarily rounding up large numbers of Jews and sending them to various concentration camps, mainly in Poland. Bendzin was very close to Oswiencim (better known as Auschwitz) concentration camp. Chilling news of what was going on there and in other camps was reaching us.

In addition, our relations with supervisor P. were deteriorating. He now had learned the business and began making our lives increasingly difficult. Many wealthy people in our town were buying foreign passports and trying to leave the country. My father was handicapped by the large size of our family. We were promised Paraguayan citizenship but only for my parents and myself. My father refused to leave the family for fear that they would perish without his protection. Little did he know that he would be powerless to protect his kinfolk. However, as I indicated previously, he was very devoted to his brothers and sisters and would not consider leaving them behind. This was not true however in reverse. Two of my father's brothers left Bendzin to fend for themselves. Ironically, both survived the war and one of them, John, married after the war and he and his wife joined us in America.

During the summer of 1943 the conditions in our province were rapidly going from bad to worse. Hitler decided on the "ultimate solution" - destruction of all Jews. Bendzin was declared "Juden Rein" - free of Jews. The entire population of Jewish inhabitants of that city was deported to Auschwitz concentration camp, one of the most feared in Poland.

A forced labor camp named Kamionka was established on the outskirts of Bendzin. Many Jewish people were expelled from their homes which were confiscated by the Nazis for resettlement of the bombed out Germans. Some of the dispossessed were incarcerated in the new camp to clean the houses of the deported Jewish population. They had to remove all the belongings, and sort them out by size and type, in preparation for distribution to the arriving Germans. After the houses were thoroughly cleaned many of the rooms were painted over and the furniture polished and neatly arranged. The houses were then ready for the arrival of the German refugees from cities devastated by the war.

Then, disaster struck. Unexpectedly, Mr. P. arranged with the local police to have the entire Fayerman family arrested. At dawn, one Sunday morning, we were aroused by loud knocking on the door and shouts of: "Open up, police here!" To our horror, the house was surrounded by men in uniform with rifles at ready. My father opened the door and was confronted by a police officer who ordered all inhabitants of the house (there were eighteen members of my father's and mother's families living together) to get dressed and step outside. Despite pleading by my father to allow us to gather some of our belongings, we were not allowed to take anything with us except the clothes we hurriedly put on. In a state of shock, we were marched to the nearby established camp of Kamionka.

Fortunately, all the family members were able to work in the camp. My mother was picked by the camp commandant to head the kitchen and house-keeping departments. This gave our family special privileges. We had a separate house in which we lived together, plenty to eat, and were allowed to pick out what we needed from the never-ending supply of goods which came from the Jewish houses. I was assigned to the house cleaning detachment. These were very easy jobs which we tried to stretch as long as possible. We knew that we would never have such good conditions in any other camp. To supplement the food rations we received from the authorities, we were allowed to requisition any food we found while emptying the houses, and we found plenty. Many people found jewelry, gold coins and foreign currencies. Most of what they found they either traded with the guards for additional amenities or buried the hoard with the intention of digging it up after the war. Kamionka soon became a veritable gold mine.

My parents' relations with the camp commandant became very cordial. We even discussed with him a plan to escape from the camp. He, however, advised us against it. The recapture percentage of the escaped prisoners was very high. As a matter of fact, all escapees from Kamionka were recaptured and summarily sent to Auschwitz for execution. The ironical part of the good relations we had with the commandant was that he told us what was in store for us. He said he thought we would probably be sent to Auschwitz as that was the closest camp. He really tried to prolong the existence of the camp as long as he could. This also secured a comfortable position for him - one which was much better than being sent to the Russian front.

However, the work of cleaning and refurbishing the former residences of the Jewish population came slowly to an end in the winter of 1943. We spent a very uneasy time not knowing where the Germans would send us from Kamionka. On January 15, 1944, the camp was closed and we were marched under military guard to the Bendzin railroad station. After several hours of waiting, a cattle train pulled into the station. Most cars were already filled with people. The train stopped and we were herded into several empty freight cars. Some tried to escape during the melee, but all were quickly recaptured. My family remained together for the last time.

We were packed tightly in a freight car which had only two small barred windows close to the roof. Father gathered everyone around him and had a long talk with us about our present situation. He said we should liken our dilemma to having been captured in a forest by bandits who might kill us all, and we had to resign ourselves to this fate. We were hoping the train was not going to Auschwitz but to a camp in Germany. Undoubtedly, these were some of the most fearful and difficult hours I ever spent. The thought of imminent death placed me in indescribable fright.

Our worst fears materialized! Our train was destined for Auschwitz. Upon arrival, we were herded out of the box cars and surrounded by SS guards with snarling dogs at their feet. An announcement was made advising elderly people, infirm, and children to wait on the side because trucks were coming to take them to the camp. Also, any mother who so chose could stay with her children. Then, the men were separated from the women.

Now the selection began for the remaining new arrivals. We were formed into lines of five persons and the first five were ordered to step forward. A doctor in SS uniform and an SS officer looked at each one briefly then motioned some to the left and some to the right. The guards then directed those individuals into two groups, the one to the right forming lines of five again and the ones to the left in a tight circle. Seeing the makeup of the two groups being formed, I instinctively understood what this meant. I removed my glasses and when ordered stepped briskly forward, stood at attention and held my breath. The doctor motioned me to the right. I was safe! I quickly moved to the next line of five forming on the side. The entire process took about half an hour.

To visually experience the selection at the trains, I recommend seeing the movie "Sophie's Choice" with Meryl Streep. It very closely depicts what occurred during that fateful late afternoon upon our arrival to Auschwitz.

The selection completed, we were marched off to the camp. By now, night had fallen. We walked alongside a muddy road with trucks passing us constantly. I noticed that the trucks were loaded with gray forms quivering on the uneven road. I wondered what they were carrying. The trucks were moving in the same direction as we were. There was no longer any daylight; it was very dark and it had started to snow. I couldn't see very far ahead. I shivered and felt the pain of fear rising within me as I realized we were now marching along a road with barbed wires on both sides. Large sentry boxes on tall wooden stands loomed every few hundred feet. Men in uniforms and helmets looked at us from every box as we passed on our slow march along the fenced road.

Finally, we stopped at a large gate. Soon another SS officer stepped out of the building near the gate. He motioned us to come forward and counted the lines of five as we passed him. This was the first of many times I would be counted during my stay in the camp. We entered the camp for the first time. By now quite a bit of snow had accumulated on the ground. We were led to a one-story wooden building and were told to sit on the floor. I looked around to see if any members of my immediate family were there. I found only two - my father and Uncle Simon. All my other relatives were absent. Soon after we were all seated a strange-looking group entered the room. They were young men dressed in dark blue and gray striped pajamas. They wore round caps without visors, which were made of the same material as their uniforms. They began moving among us. They asked if we had any money or jewelry and told us to give it to them because soon an SS guard would arrive and confiscate all we had. I had some money and I approached one of the men promising him payment if he would tell me where we were and what was going to happen to us.

He was a nice young man with a pleasant smile. He sat beside me and told me we were in Auschwitz II or the camp called Birkenau. He said I was a lucky man to be alive as the rest of the people in our group (all the others who had arrived that afternoon) had been gassed and would be cremated that night. I asked with parched lips, "And the women, what did they do with them?" He

7

answered, "The able-bodied and young ones were taken to the women's camp and are undergoing the same process as you. Soon you will have to give up all your clothes, and you will get a number which they will tattoo on your left arm. You will be given a shower, clothes like I am wearing, and you will spend the night here. In the morning they will transfer you to the quarantine camp."

I gave him all the money I had except several marks and my wrist watch. I thought just in case he was not telling the truth it would be prudent to have some valuables on me. But, just as he said, a few minutes later an SS guard entered, told us to line up and to empty our pockets on a nearby table. I did exactly as he instructed. Soon the table was full of wallets, money, rings and watches. The guard inspected all very thoroughly and threatened that if he found anything on us, even a pocket knife, the guilty would be shot right there. Then, he did find some paper bills on one man. He ordered him to undress and stood him naked by the wall. He took his pistol and placed it at the poor man's temple. The victim turned all colors - first red, then blue and gray, then white, and back to red. The guard kept the pistol at his head for several moments. Then he replaced it in his holster and told the man he was lucky this time. Suddenly, additional valuables were furtively placed on the table.

Shortly the same young men who came in first reappeared. They told us to undress to our waist and form three lines. The tattooing began. I stood behind my father and uncle. My father was first and he got the number 171949; my uncle was next, his number was 171950. Suddenly, a commotion occurred and an SS guard dragged a reluctant man to be tattooed next. I followed and received the number 171952, which I still have on my left forearm. This small incident is important to the rest of my story.

The tattooing hurt. I bled from the punctures but I was so terrified of what was going on around me that I was oblivious to the pain. The tattooing completed, we were moved to another room where we were told to undress completely and climb on a stool one by one. Then all the hair on our bodies was shaved. Next, the barbers arrived and shaved everyone's head. The only hair remaining on my body was the eyebrows and eyelashes. I felt nothing by then. I just wanted this ordeal and debasement to end quickly. Naked and shivering, with a bleeding forearm, I entered a large shower room. First I had to climb into a vat containing a bluish liquid. A man quickly pushed my head under the water and then let me go. (This was to rid us of any possibility of lice.) I climbed out and went under the shower. There was a piece of soap for everyone. The hot shower felt good on my wet and cold body. Soon the showers stopped and we were rushed to another room where they gave us towels. After drying ourselves, we deposited the towels into a basket and proceeded to a bench where clothing was distributed. I was again lucky. The same young prisoner to whom I had given money came to me and took me behind the benches. There he picked new clothes for me, which fit me well, and gave me a pair of shoes identical to his. They were ankle high leather with wooden soles. I had to get used to walking in them.

We were then returned to the room we had entered when we first arrived at the barracks. Our group was now alone except for a family sitting against the wall. I was surprised to see them and couldn't figure out what they were doing there. They were still dressed in their fine, civilian clothing. There was a man who appeared to be the head of the family, his wife, several other adults and children. I approached one of the family members and asked him what they were doing there. He didn't understand Polish. I then asked him in German, then French. It was obvious by his reaction that he understood French, but he only spoke Italian. He said to leave them alone and not come any closer. He looked at us with loathing and fear.

Later, I learned that they were an important Italian Jewish family of high standing and had been brought to the camp by car, arriving late that same evening. For some unknown reason, the Germans played a charade with important prisoners. They were treated very politely, although their fate had already been decided. The guards included the family with the next day's contingent to the gas chambers.

I hardly slept that first night in the camp. Huddled close to my father and uncle, I drifted in and out of a fitful sleep. In the morning, we were lined up, counted and then marched off. While marching to our assigned barracks, I noticed the camp was actually made up of many compounds which were separated by barbed wire and had their own contingent of guards. We were assigned to a barrack in the middle of the camp. It was a long wooden structure resembling a military installation. Through the center, the entire length of the building, was a long brick structure, which actually was a heating oven. At the far end of the building there was a chimney which went through the roof.

Alongside the roof line were windows which ran almost the length of the building. It was murky inside the barracks but my eyes soon got accustomed to the semi-darkness. We were greeted by our section leader (called Capo) who was dressed in a dark navy suit made to look like our pajamas. He wore nice riding boots. I discovered later that he was a German criminal removed from a prison and assigned to supervise us.

The Capo instructed us on our daily chores during our quarantine, which consisted of our keeping our sleeping berth clean and tidy, and told us the basic rules. He ordered us to find ourselves a place to sleep which would be our permanent spot until we were moved to our next assignment. A scramble ensued and I managed to grab a spot for me, my father and uncle on the middle tier of the sleeping berth. After settling in and placing my blanket on my sleeping berth, I had a chance to look around and get acquainted with the place of my incarceration. It was a wooden barracks with room for approximately 300 people, although the authorities managed to crowd more in at various times. Through the center, as I indicated previously, ran a heating stove. On both sides of the building were three tiers of berths, resembling large size shelving. On the bottom of each shelf was a sack filled with straw on which men lay 10 to each shelf. Thus, in one unit there were thirty men. There was space between each unit for the occupants to climb in and out. In addition to the blanket, each person was given one metal bowl and a cup and spoon. These were all of our earthly belongings. We guarded them with our lives. I managed to attach the utensils to my clothing in order to carry them with me when away from the barracks.

The purpose of placing us in the quarantine barracks was to get us used to the food and environment as well as having us available for various work assignments. The average day would begin at 5:00 a.m. with the ringing of a bell and our block-chief standing ready with a whip. It was still dark and very cold. Half naked, we were herded out of the barracks to an outside latrine and washroom which was approximately 20 yards away. We were given one small

stepped up to the high-tension wires to be electrocuted. Many became feeble and very thin. Every day the guards would come to our barracks asking for a number of workers to perform labor-intensive chores in and out of camp. All had to line up and stand to be counted. Almost every time this happened, the Capo would come out of his office and pull me out of the line to stay behind, claiming that I was needed in the barracks. Soon I became known as the Englishman. The guards would joke, asking me if I was parachuted into the camp. I laughed with them, particularly because I didn't have to go to work except dusting the Capo's apartment. I wasn't always lucky; it depended on the urgency of the work to be performed or the number of available prisoners.

The outside work was hard. We were taken to dig long ditches which were used for burying dead prisoners and ashes from the crematoriums. Sometimes the guards were violent and would beat the slower-moving men or prod them to work faster. The men were weak and many were unsuited for this type of labor. Some fell from exhaustion and we had to carry them back to the camp where we laid them on the ground next to us to be counted. The next morning they were gone. Now I understood what the masses of gray quivering matter were on the trucks the night we arrived at the camp. They were the collected dead bodies from various camps being taken to the crematoriums.

One day when the Capo had me stay in the barracks while the majority of the inmates went outside to work, I heard a bell ringing and the shouted order that no one was to leave the barracks. Wondering what was happening, I went outside and hid behind a garbage bin. It was very quiet and I waited, perhaps fifteen minutes, and then decided to go back inside as the cold rain and wind soaked my thin striped uniform. Suddenly, however, from the direction of the women's camp, I heard a woman screaming wildly, and then to my horror I saw the reason for her screams. Large trucks loaded with naked women were being driven toward the crematorium. I counted fifteen trucks, some with trailers, carrying 40 or 45 women each. Soon the screaming stopped and the trucks returned empty, to bring new victims to the furnaces. Four times those convoys of death passed by me. On the fifth trip, a young girl in her early twenties jumped from a truck in an attempt to escape, but fell on the ground and looked helplessly around. She was naked and shivering. A

13

passing SS guard on a motorcycle saw her, stopped, got off his vehicle and ran up to her. The woman crossed her arms over her breast and cried, "Shoot me. I beg you to kill me!" He laughed loudly and kicked her in the stomach and then jumped on her body and continued stomping on her until she ceased to move. The mud was mixed with her blood. The next truck took the dirty corpse to the furnaces. Horrified and sickened, I ran back to my barracks as quickly as I could.

As the barracks became less and less crowded because of the high mortality rate of the prisoners, new waves of men were arriving. The most notable was a large group of Greeks. They were guerillas caught by the Germans during the uprising in the Balkans. Approximately two hundred were assigned to our barracks. After one month only three were still present at countdown. One of them was a boxer and the other two were fishermen. The main problem the Greek prisoners had was that they couldn't stand the cold weather. Most of them caught colds which spread rapidly between them because of the close quarters in which we lived, and many were severely beaten by the guards because they couldn't understand the commands for work.

The most dreaded occurrence at the camp was the so-called "selection," which was scheduled every two months. On that fateful day, no one was sent to work. Before noon the SS doctor and several guards arrived. We were told to undress completely and move to one side of the barracks. The doctor stood by the entrance door. We were ordered to come forward one by one, stand at attention and turn around when so directed. With a motion of his hand, the doctor would indicate to each of us to either cross over to the other side of the heating stove or come forward to him. The crossover meant we were allowed to continue our miserable existence. To come forward meant a guard would grab the unfortunate man's hand and read aloud his number, which was recorded by another clerk. Some protested and implored the doctor to let them cross over with the others. Their pleading was to no avail. The doctor's face was stern and he showed no emotion. When the selection was completed, the SS left.

An unbelievable feeling of shock and horror overwhelmed all. I didn't comprehend at first the meaning of this bizarre procedure, but slowly I realized that I had witnessed a drama in which men were sentenced to die. Three days later we were again ordered not to leave the barracks. This time a contingent of guards arrived. One of them called out numbers, the prisoners whose numbers were announced slowly stepped forward. The numbers were verified, the clerk checked them off, and the men were ordered to leave the barracks and line up outside.

It was then that the most moving episode occurred, which I remember clearly to this day. A father of one of my school friends was called, as he knew he would be. He had been a tall handsome man but was now haggard and wrinkled. He walked past me, stood in the aisle and in a lugubrious voice said, "Avenge my innocent death! Kill the German bastards!" Defiantly he walked up to the clerk and slowly left the barracks.

I don't know why this incident left such a deep impression in my memory. I saw far greater atrocities in the camp, but somehow I never forgot this dreadful incident. Right then and there I swore to avenge these poor victims. I gave my pledge, my word of honor. But somehow, after the war, I couldn't go through with the promise of avenging them. Killing others would not bring my friends back. I couldn't, of course, take anyone's life. Instead, I promised to never erase the tattoo from my arm. This would become for the rest of my life a badge of honor.

One of the most exhausting duties in the camp was the evening counting of all the prisoners. We were counted over and over again during each day. First thing in the morning after breakfast we had to file outside the barracks to be counted. When we were leaving the camp for work assignments we were counted out. Upon return from work we were counted once more. But the worst was the evening count. Regardless of the weather, as evening fell, all prisoners had to line up outside the barracks to be counted. We would stand for hours in the cold, rain or snow. It was an ordeal which many could not survive. Sometimes the guards would miscount and return to every group to count the prisoners again. This went on until the commandant was satisfied with the count. During this procedure we had to stand perfectly still. However, in order to get through this ordeal, when the guard left with his count, I would move my feet rapidly to get warm and talk to myself to mentally escape from the pain and discomfort. Occasionally, there was an escape and the sirens would sound to alert the chain of guards who surrounded the camps.

Inevitably the following day upon our return to the camp, we would see the escapees either standing inside the gate with their hands and legs tied, or hanging from the gallows. The punishment for trying to escape was death by hanging. Often the entire camp population was ordered to witness the hanging as a warning to all. Attempts to escape were very rare.

We also were ordered to witness corporal punishment for smaller infractions, such as stealing food, bribing the guards, or avoiding work details. The unfortunate recipient of the punishment was tied to a tall four-legged bench. Each limb was then tethered to one of the bench legs and a guard would mete the blows. Another prisoner was assigned to count loudly each stroke of the whip, which was followed by the shriek of the victim. Twenty-five strokes was the minimum punishment, however, fifty strokes was more common.

I saw guards perform many unbelievably sadistic acts of atrocity, about which I cannot elaborate because it is too upsetting for me.

I only want to tell about one incident which, sad as it was, under different circumstances would have been comical to watch. We had one guard, a tall and burly SS man, who in civilian life had been a dentist. Every other week there was one Sunday off from work. The prisoners had one day of leisure, usually spent milling around the camp trying to procure extra food or clothing. The "Dentist" would stride into the main road of the camp and call for a passing prisoner to come to him. The prisoner, of course, had to obey. The "Dentist" would ask the unfortunate man if he had a toothache. Regardless of the answer, he ordered the man to open his mouth. After grabbing him tightly around his head, he would pull out a tooth with dental pincers he always kept hidden from view. Then, laughing, he would let the bleeding man go, saying, "This tooth will hurt you no more."

The trick was to stay away from the SS "'Dentist" and be alert at all times. This was the way to survive in the camp. Most of the victims were newcomers to the camp or worn out prisoners who became lethargic and were entering the final stage of their life in the camp. They were dubbed "Muslims." They were emaciated human beings who looked like the Hindu Fakirs. They moved slowly; their eyes were large and deeply set in the sockets. Within a week or so, they would most probably fall to the ground at one of the evening roll calls and be taken away that very night.

I was determined to avoid becoming a "Muslim" at all costs. I had to get more food and avoid hard outside labor. My Capo saw to it that I stayed in the camp most of the time; consequently, I had plenty of opportunity to look around. We were quartered next to a gypsy camp where entire families lived together in common barracks. They were never ordered to go to work but seemed to live a life such as they would have on the outside, except that they, like us, were prisoners. Still, we considered them lucky. They kept their civilian clothing, seemed to be well fed, and had their entire families with them. They, too, however, eventually fell victim to the death camp, as one day they were all gone. Apparently the Germans needed the barracks in which they were housed and killed them.

Two barracks away from mine was a strange-looking structure resembling ours but painted dark red. The doors to this barrack were always closed. At regular intervals a group of prisoners would emerge from the building, line up outside and then march off to work like any other group, except they were well-dressed and well-fed men. I was told this was the crematorium detachment. I don't know why I was fascinated by them. Maybe because they reminded me of the Roman gladiators - destined to die sooner or later. After a given period, the men became crazed from doing this horrendous work and the guards would kill them. Then during one of the selections, a new crew would be picked to take the place of the slain predecessors. I prayed not to be picked for the crematorium detail.

One day as I was standing by the side watching the prisoners as they arrived to their red barracks, I spotted a friend I knew from school. I called to him and walked alongside. His name was John Stolica. He carried a sack slung over his shoulder. He recognized me and asked what I was doing. After I told him he smiled faintly and said I was lucky. John must have understood that I was hungry and he tossed a half of a loaf of bread to me; I caught it, thanked him and continued to march alongside. He said, "Be here tomorrow and I will bring more food." Soon he disappeared inside the red barrack.

What luck, I thought, but my friends warned me to stay clear of the commando as it was forbidden for other prisoners to have contact with the crematorium group. I didn't pay any attention - I was not going to become a "Muslim" - I had to get more food. And, so it was for the next several days. I would wait for the crematorium group to get back and my friend would toss bundles of food to me. All good things come to an end, and, to my utter dismay, my friend John was moved to another shift.

I wouldn't, couldn't, give up that easily, however. I decided to sneak into the red barrack and seek my friend who would be sleeping during the day as he was now on the night shift. There was a smaller side door to the building, usually leading to Capo's quarters. I tried the door. It wasn't locked. I entered the red barrack with great trepidation. There was the usual semi-darkness inside the building and walls were painted in the same dark color as the outside. On the commodious bunks were laying men, most of them unclad and snoring loudly. I walked quickly looking for my friend but to no avail. I stood silently, looking cautiously all around. A strange and heavy atmosphere prevailed everywhere. I noticed a pair of dark piercing eyes looking at me. The man softly called to me; I approached hesitantly. He was a large man. He asked me what I was doing there and I told him I was looking for my friend John Stolica. He didn't seem to know him. "You know," he said, "if they catch you inside this building, you may never leave." I told him I was hungry. He reached behind him and lifted a whole sack of what I found later to be a mixture of rolls, sausage and a jar full of lard. "Take it," he said, "and get out of here and don't ever come back."

Quickly, I obeyed his admonition. I found my way out and happily returned to my barracks. There was enough food for my father, uncle, and me for a long time as we supplemented our rations with this wonderful gift. I will always remember this eerie experience in the red barrack. It exemplifies the risks one had to take in order to try to survive another day.

During the fifth week of our imprisonment an event occurred which would save our lives. An announcement was made that anyone with bookkeeping and mechanical engineering experience should apply at the main camp office. My father and my uncle applied. They were gone for several hours. Upon their return, my father told me they were both accepted and would be leaving soon for an unknown destination. I was happy for them but saddened by the fact that we would be separated and I would have to fend for myself. In about three days my father and my Uncle Simon left after a heart-breaking goodbye. My father reminded me that if we survived, our meeting place would be great-grandmother's house outside of Salzburg. I had tears in my eyes when I saw them leaving the prison gate.

Now I was really alone but I kept very busy. Between tending to my bene-factor and teaching the Capo, a good part of the day went by. In my spare time, I would saunter around the camp looking for an opportunity to earn extra food.

My turn to leave the camp came soon after my family left. An announce-ment was made that they were looking for tool and die makers. I applied and in two days I was called to the main office. There was a group of about twenty other prisoners to be interviewed. I waited until a good friend of mine was called. When he emerged, I questioned him about the examination. He fully explained what they questioned him about. It sounded very simple. Next was my turn. I walked into a room simply furnished. Two men in civilian clothes and one SS officer were sitting at a table facing the door. On my left stood a table with various metal objects. I walked up briskly, took off my cap and stood at attention in a military fashion. The SS officer spoke first: "You will be asked questions about how to make tools. If you are here under false pretenses you will be punished by assignment into the mines." Work in the mines was the most dreaded fate. No one ever came back from this most inhumane and dangerous work to which the Germans subjected their prisoners. I nodded and in a clear and loud tone said, "I understand."

One of the civilians showed me a blueprint and asked me to explain what it was for. I answered promptly and firmly. He nodded and took me over to a table on which lay several stamping tools and metal parts. Again he ques-tioned me about what the objects were. The last question pertained to how I would make a tool for a relatively simple part resembling a washer. I explained in detail. The other man interrupted and asked how I would calculate the clearance between the punch and the die. When I was finished answering, he got up, grinned, and said to the others, "We want this one."

Thus, I was hired by Siemens-Schuckert Electric Company whose successor is Siemens A.C. They are the largest manufacturer of electrical products in Germany, producing a whole range of electrical equipment now distributed in the United States. I am very grateful to Siemens; undoubtedly, by hiring me, they saved my life.

All twenty applicants were hired. In a week we were called back to the office and a civilian in the presence of the camp commandant informed us we would be starting work in a few days. Unfortunately, the plant was not ready. We were assigned to renovating an old flour mill and converting it into a modern plant. Machinery would then be installed and we would begin our work as tool and die makers. Wonderful news. We were to start work on the next Monday, but before this good turn of events, I experienced another terrible thing. We were warned by "old numbers" that from time to time the SS would empty entire sections of the camp and send all indiscriminately to the gas chambers. On the Saturday before our work at Siemens was to begin, we were told there would be no work assignments that day. Shortly after breakfast, a large contingent of guards arrived at our camp. They closed off several barracks and ordered all out. They marched us to a large empty building opposite the main entrance to the camp. The empty building was eventually filled so that only standing room remained. The doors were closed and guards posted outside.

It was dark inside the building. In the gloom of the barrack the prisoners began to speculate. It looked like one of the camp "cleaning actions" which was the wholesale removal of one group of prisoners to make room for others arriving on the train. I can't begin to describe my state of mind. To this day, when I think about it I can still feel the terror. Many began to pray and recite the psalms for the dead. I wanted to find a small hole into which I could crawl to hide from the terrible fate which awaited us. My thoughts raced seeking a way out. Maybe Siemens would come to the rescue, and I would be saved. For the first time in a very long time, I began to pray.

I lost track of time. I don't remember how long we were in the dark building. Suddenly, the doors opened and the bright sunlight blinded me. I heard the guards yelling at us in their usual coarse manner: "All out! Quickly!" adding the usual swear words which always accompanied their barked orders. We fearfully went outside, standing around bewildered and frightened. "Back to your barracks, you dogs!" was the next command. I ran as fast as I could. When we all returned to our assigned barracks, we tried to speculate on what had happened. Of course no one knew. Only later did I find out the course of events.

A new trainload of people had arrived at the camp but there was no room for them. The head office in Auschwitz ordered our commandant of Birkenau to empty as many barracks as necessary to house the new arrivals. The quarantine had to be cleared. I am not sure what or who intervened. Was it the fact that a number of prisoners in my camp were awaiting transfer to various other jobs and camps, or that our commandant prevailed that it was simpler to exterminate the new group rather than the already processed inmates of his camp? I don't know, but others were sacrificed which in turn saved our lives.

Siemens Camp

This opens a new chapter of my experiences at Birkenau, a satellite camp to Auschwitz. I am using the German names because Birkenau was a creation of the Nazis.

Actually the Siemens plant was in existence at the time we were hired by Siemens' officials. The site was occupied by a large complex of factory buildings dating back to the late 1800s. The property consisted of about ten acres, located approximately five miles from Birkenau.

Every morning our group, which was named "The Siemens Commando," lined up outside our barracks. We were counted again and allowed to leave the gate. Outside there were several military personnel carriers. We would climb inside the carriers and the guards were placed at the drop gates of the trucks. Thus, we traveled in relative comfort to the work site. This was a great advantage, I might add, because many other prisoners had to walk several miles every day to their assigned work details and back to the camp after a hard day's work.

On our first day of work we began to rebuild the old plant in which our future operation would be housed. The new camp commandant told us the sooner we finished the job of preparing the factory, the sooner we would start our work as tool makers. The incentive was of course to work harder and faster rebuilding the plant so that we could have an easier job inside.

Thus began the tedious job of clearing the old buildings of accumulated rubbish. Best preserved were the office buildings where our new camp commandant lived with all the guards and where Siemens opened their executive offices. The actual plant, which consisted of two large brick buildings and a power plant, was about 1,000 yards away. This was a common arrangement

23

of industrial complexes at the beginning of the 20th century. One of the one-story high brick buildings was being converted into the manufacturing operation. The other multi-story structure was adapted to living quarters for us. We were aided by a group of female prisoners from Birkenau. These women were actually part of the construction crew supplied by the camp administration. As luck would have it, I was overjoyed to learn that they were housed in the same barracks as my mother. I thus established contact with her. I had plenty of food and would often send her packages which the girls would smuggle into the camp upon their return every evening. Mother would write to me and at least I knew she was well. She was assigned to a munitions factory outside the camp. The German industrials established various factories near the camp profiting by the cheap and abundant labor.

We established that my mother and I were crossing paths each morning. She would march to work and we would pass the moving columns of prisoners on our way to the Siemens Plant. I passed a note to her describing our trucks and asked her to take off her kerchief in order for me to recognize her among the hundreds of other women all dressed alike, looking like gray ghosts in the damp early morning. I had come to be on very good terms with our guards and I asked if they would let me stand at the tailgate so that I could spot my mother.

The trucks would usually slow down as we were passing the marching columns of prisoners. This would give me time to quickly scan the gray clad inmates. I was not always lucky but on a few occasions I would get a fleeting glance of my mother. One time, as luck would have it, the truck stopped and the column of women caught up to us. When I spotted my mother I began waving my cap. She rushed forward and called, "My baby. My baby!" I nearly fell out of the truck leaning out to touch her. The guards held me back while the girls around my mother gave way so she could come closer to me. An indescribable scene occurred. Everyone suddenly realized that a son had found his mother in the middle of the inferno called Auschwitz. There was a hush, and a long silence followed as the truck slowly picked up speed and my mother tried to follow, being restrained by her fellow prisoners.

I was moved to tears and no one spoke a word all the way to the work site.

Later, the guards from my truck walked up to me and told me they would try to stop the truck anytime I could spot my mother. To me, this demonstrated that there is some good in almost everyone. I was fortunate to spot my mother several times during our trips to work. In some instances, the guards were able to persuade the driver to slow down so that we could at least look at one another.

However, the opportunity to see my mother ceased when the construction phase ended and we remained permanently at the Siemens camp. I completely lost contact with her as we were isolated with no means of communication with the rest of Birkenau. But, at this time, a most fortunate period of my story in the concentration camps began. On the first morning of our installation at the new camp, we were gathered and the camp commandant started selecting a housekeeping group. My best friend and barrack buddy was picked to be the assistant cook. What luck! We slept next to one another on the top shelf with all the "camp celebrities," namely: cooks, the medical team and other men performing important work in the plant. Naturally, he had all the food he could eat in the kitchen but every evening he would steal some for me.

Some of the girls who came to work during construction of the plant were selected to clean the offices and serve food to the guards and office employees. They also operated the staff kitchen. One of the Polish girls named Bronia befriended me. The women were housed in an adjoining building and fraternization was forbidden; however, at the end of each day all the prisoners were allowed free time outside of their sleeping quarters. The guards would look the other way when we approached a fence separating the two buildings. There at least we could have contact with the girls. Bronia would nearly always tuck away some food in her apron. She would seek me out and pass the morsels of whatever was left from the tables.

It is difficult to imagine the perseverance of the human race. Under the most adverse circumstances people seek one another and form friendships and build ties, even as death stares them in the face. It simply proves the point that we are naturally gregarious beings who unite in the presence of mortal danger, although we may be helpless to save one another. Particularly among the young people there seemed to be a powerful strength which helped them keep going no matter what happened around them.

Finally, the job of preparing the buildings was finished and we began our work inside the plant. We were separated into various groups: machinists, bench fitters and general laborers. I applied for bench fitting work and was given a difficult test piece to execute. My supervisor was impressed. He called me aside and we had a lengthy talk. He offered me a job as tool layout mechanic. I was given a bench at the head of the tool and die department. There I would review each order as it was received in the plant. The orders consisted of a set of plans to make dies and tools and I would requisition the proper pieces of tool steel for each set of plans. Then the blueprints and pieces of steel were placed on a cart. The supervisor would then assign the building of a particular tool to a group of tool and die makers. This was a responsible job, plus it gave me an opportunity to walk all over the plant and familiarize myself with all of the latest tool-making machinery. I actually perfected my skill of tool making at this very modern plant belonging to one of the largest manufacturing giants in the world. The work was a tonic to our nerves and afforded us an avenue of escape from the monotony of the imprisonment.

I must have impressed my German civilian supervisor because he treated me with civility and kindness. On many days when I arrived at work in the morning and opened my tool box there would be something to eat in it. Only my boss had access to all the tool boxes; therefore, I was confident he was giving me extra bits of food from his own food ration.

Our camp commandant was of Polish extraction. He chose to become a "Volks Deutche" which means he relinquished Polish citizenship and opted to become a German national. Many Silesians did this. It benefited their entire family as they were given the same privileges as the German nationals; however, able-bodied men had to sign up with the German army. Most were not fully trusted by the German authorities; consequently, they were placed in positions not requiring front line duties and often assigned to guard prisoners. Our commandant was an easy-going man. He spoke German to us but we knew he could speak and understand Polish very well. He had a friend who was always present when trains arrived with new prisoners. In almost all cases the prisoners brought food with them for their journey. This they were made to leave behind just as I had to upon my arrival to the camp. This fellow would then load a car full of the confiscated food and bring it to our camp for distribution. It gave us an opportunity to taste some of the best bread, sausage and marmalade from all parts of Eastern Europe. We all realized that we were benefiting from the misfortune of others but we were grateful for the opportunity to fill our stomachs. After all, we rationalized, the people who originally brought the food to the camp no longer needed it. A very callous way of justifying our acceptance of this manna from the trains, but the hunger and the will to survive was stronger than any of our scruples. I must admit I gained weight and prospered.

The summer came with its warm and pleasant days. On the free days, I would lie in the grass staring at the blue skies, forgetting my misfortune. It's hard to believe, but it was a time that I was relatively happy and content in this oasis surrounded by a sea of suffering.

The Letter

One evening in the summer of 1944 as I was meeting Bronia, she told me that one of the girls had seen a letter addressed to me on the desk of the camp commandant. I was shocked at hearing this news and wondered how I could obtain it. I decided to wait a few days hoping the commandant would bring it to me, however, to no avail. Several days later after the evening roll call, I stepped up to the commandant and asked about the letter. The commandant looked at me for a few seconds then turned on his heels and walked away without saying a word. When I mentioned my unsuccessful attempt to obtain the letter to Bronia, she confirmed that the letter was still in the office. One week went by, then the fateful day came on Tuesday. I was working at my bench fully absorbed in what I was doing when I felt a slight tap on my shoulder. I turned around and there was one of the guards ordering me to follow him. My supervisor, who was nearby, nodded, indicating that he was aware of my being taken away from work.

I apprehensively followed the guard to the main office building. I distinctly remember the walk; it was a beautiful warm day, not a cloud in the sky. We walked along a path which led through a lush green meadow into woods where the offices were located. I was afraid of what might happen next. I was admitted to the camp commandant's office. Behind his desk sat two SS officers. Our commandant stood near the door. I walked in briskly, stood at attention and removed my cap in a formal military fashion. One of the SS officers asked me my name and number. He then handed me an open letter and asked me to read it. It was from my father. I recognized his very fine and legible handwriting. It was rather brief and read as follows: "Dear Severin, I and Simon (my uncle) are well and doing fine. We are worried about you and mother. Do you know where she is? Did you see her? Are you able to help her? Try to be brave. We hope to see you after the war. Keep well. Your loving Father."

After I read and reread the letter I gave it back to the SS officer, thanking him for letting me read it. I managed a faint smile but remained standing at attention. The same officer who gave me the letter got up and came around the desk. He slapped my cheeks shouting "Take that smile off of your face," and added a few other choice words. Then he asked me who wrote the letter. I explained it was from my father. "How did he know you are here?" he asked. I replied, "He was sent to another camp and this is the first time I ever heard from him." Then he asked me where my mother was. I told him I didn't know, that we were separated when we came to Auschwitz. He slapped me again shouting that I was lying. He also asked how often I received letters and how I communicated with my mother. I replied that I had told him all I knew. He slapped me again and ordered me to turn around and bend over. I felt a sharp blow of a stiff object on my buttocks. I clenched my teeth and didn't utter a sound. The second blow came, and then a third, and on and on he continued beating me. I don't remember how long it was until I could no longer stand it and began to cry in pain after every blow. A few minutes passed by and I knew I wouldn't be able to stand this punishment much longer. I fell to the floor moaning in pain: "May the Lord be my witness, I am telling the truth."

The beating stopped. The SS officer turned to our camp commandant and asked him to translate what I had just said. The men talked amongst themselves for a few minutes. Then one returned to me, looked at my prostrate body on the floor and poured a cup of cold coffee on me. I pretended to come back to life. One of them said, "You are faking it, don't try to fool us. Get up and get out of here."

I left the room as quickly as I could and limped back to my bench. Everyone was looking at me as I returned to work. I was stained with coffee and my face was red. Automatically, I picked up a file, placed a piece of steel in the vise and carefully and very professionally began to file. In a little while, I realized that the same SS men who interrogated me had come to inspect the plant. Before leaving, they stood behind me observing what I was doing. For a few minutes they talked to my supervisor and, finally, they left. Absentmindedly, I continued to file for a long time, trying not to think about the terrible, frightening events of that dreadful day.

That evening my buddy inspected my buttocks. There were wide and deep welts all over. The camp doctor administered a salve. I had to lay on my stomach at night and I couldn't sit down for a long time.

The weeks went by and the work and life routine continued, and I nearly forgot about that unpleasant incident. Then at the end of one working day, my supervisor told me I was to be transferred back to Auschwitz. I was horrified and pleaded with him to let me stay, but he said there was nothing he could do about it - I would be leaving Siemens camp the next morning.

In a state of dread, I lay awake most of the night. The consensus was that I was going to my execution for receiving the letter. This, I was told, was the punishment for any infraction in the camp. I was not allowed to receive letters and I supposedly was suspected of wrongdoing. The next morning at dawn, I gathered my meager belongings and said farewell to my buddy and friends. A guard came to fetch me; we walked in the cool, wet morning to the main office building. There was a staff car waiting. I got inside. To my surprise, my supervisor came in and sat next to me. On the other side sat the guard. Next to the driver was the camp commandant. We drove in silence.

When we arrived at the main entrance to Auschwitz I noticed a large sign spanning the gate with this wording: "Work makes you free." I was told to get out and stand by the gate. The guard stood with me in complete silence. After about a half hour, which seemed like an eternity, my escorts returned. They approached me saying, "You have to stay here. We tried to keep you but to no avail. There is an order from Berlin requesting your transfer." Before getting back into the staff car, my supervisor said goodbye and good luck.

I waited for about an hour. Then a guard came to me and motioned for me to follow him. I was processed in the registration office and assigned to the transient barracks. What an indescribable relief. I was not going to be executed but transferred somewhere else. Well, whatever the fate may be, I was still alive and that was all that mattered.

The transient camp was a large multi-story red brick building, one of the nicest in Auschwitz. This was actually the first time I was admitted to the main camp. I didn't venture too far into the camp, as I feared this monstrous killing institution. I was assigned to a single bed on the third floor of a building which resembled a hospital. There were several large rooms on each floor. Each room was filled with single beds with ample room between them. I thought I was in a luxury hotel in comparison with the usual camp accommodations. The food was much better than in the camp and we had free time all day.

After a few days, I began to be bored and wanted something to do. There was a tall man in the same room with me who was respected by all. He had a large bed with plenty of open space around it. I figured he must be someone special. In my usual manner, I walked up to him and asked if he needed a servant. He said, yes, that he didn't have anyone at present and I could do his clothing. I remembered the routine from the quarantine camp and began washing his clothes, mending his socks and making his bed. For this, every day he brought me a full loaf of bread and a large piece of sausage. He told me to help myself to as much margarine and jam as I wanted. He ordered a new outfit for me and brought me a new pair of boots. I thought I was in heaven. Then someone finally informed me that he was the camp executioner and feared by everyone. They couldn't understand why he had taken a liking to me. The reason really didn't matter to me, I was busy. I was eating royally and I was alive! At that time, that was all that mattered to me. I was just trying to survive.

New men were constantly coming and leaving the transient barracks. I awaited my turn with great anticipation. But, nothing happened. A week went by, and then another and another. I was still there. I asked my benefactor to find out what was in store for me. He inquired and was told the same thing I already knew; i.e., there was an order from Berlin for my transfer. I thought this was very strange. More weeks went by and still nothing happened.

Then one day a young German Jew arrived to our barracks. He was being transferred from Sachsenhausen near Berlin to a camp in Breslau. We had plenty of time on our hands and he told me a lot about himself. I told him my story to which he listened in near disbelief. While I was talking he kept observing me attentively. He asked me about my father. With a strange look on his face he said, "I now understand the whole story. You are going to Sachsenhausen - where I just came from." He told me that my father and uncle were in a special secret commando at Sachsenhausen, a huge concentration camp outside of Berlin where many political prisoners were being kept. He went on to tell me that Stalin's son Jacob was there as well as the prime minister of France and many high dignitaries from countries conquered by Germany. They were kept in a separate section of the camp and treated much better than the rest of the inmates. Heinrich Himmler, the infamous German Secretary of the Interior, who was the engineer of the German extermination machine, set up a special secret camp within Sachsenhausen in order to produce false documents to be used by the German Military Intelligence.

After the war my father told me that he and my Uncle Simon were employed as a bookkeeper and engineer respectively. The bookkeeping consisted of keeping tabs on the counterfeit currency serial numbers and the engineering was to keep the very specialized printing presses in good working condition. My father gained the confidence of the camp commandant. He was allowed outside of the secret camp in order to accompany sick prisoners to the camp hospital. (That's where he met my new friend.) Having gained the trust of his superiors, he implored them to bring me to the special camp.

All prisoners were identified by the number tattooed on their arm. Thus, to arrange the transfer my father needed to give them my number. He mistakenly gave them number 171951, which was in fact the number of the reluctant man the guards forcibly put between my uncle and me to be tattooed that first night of our imprisonment. Consequently, to my father's dismay, in place of me a young man with a fully shaven head arrived at Sachsenhausen. My father was distraught but didn't give up. He prevailed to have the commandant send another transfer request, this time with the correct number; namely, 171952.

My new friend assured me that the life in the special camp was the best possible and that I would be lucky to go there. One word of warning he added, however, before leaving for his destination near Breslau. He said he felt that no one from the special camp would survive the war as the Germans would not want the world to know what went on in that camp. Well, I was left with many heavy thoughts. On one hand, I was very worried about the eventual fate of my father and my favorite uncle, Simon, and wanted to be with them. On the other hand, I had a very nice life at Siemens, of which my father, of course, was not aware. He wanted to save me as he thought I was lingering in Birkenau, most probably doing hard labor, which I would not be able to endure very long. In the meantime, nothing was happening to me. I continued my routine life in the transitional camp.

One early fall day a large contingent of young Frenchmen arrived, destined for the Siemens camp. I was able to tell them all about the life in the camp to which they were assigned. A few days later the Frenchmen were called to assemble in the yard for transfer to Siemens. I accompanied them in order to say my farewell. The new Siemens group consisted of twenty-seven men. The guards who were to escort them to the camp had a list of twenty-eight prisoners, one was missing. They kept counting and recounting the men, unable to reconcile the number with their list. One guard went back to the barracks to check if anyone was left behind. Several minutes elapsed. Being a transient camp, men were moved in and out on a daily basis. Compared to the other camps it was loosely structured and no one would question what happened to one prisoner. They would simply assume he had been transferred. So, it occurred to me it was my chance to sneak back to the old camp. I simply stepped in line with the rest of the French prisoners. The guard returned from his search of the barracks and started counting again with me in the line. Twenty-eight prisoners present and accounted for he reported to his superiors. "Out with you all," shouted the impatient officer in charge and, thus, I simply walked out of Auschwitz back to Siemens.

My friends at the camp couldn't believe their eyes when I walked in with the new group. I was clad in clean new pajamas and wearing a beautiful pair of shoes. Unfortunately, I left all the good food behind me but I consoled myself that it was worth losing the food for the return to Siemens. I was given back my old job and, considering the circumstances, continued a relatively happy existence in this exceptional working camp.

I never learned what happened to my transfer to Sachsenhausen, although later my father told me Siemens Company was adamant about keeping me and didn't want to give me up. It is possible that my supervisor knew I was still in Auschwitz and when the new contingent of French prisoners arrived he added one more to the list, hoping I would be included.

Fall turned to winter. In the spring of 1944 good news was reaching us. The Americans landed in Normandy. Paris was liberated - our Frenchmen rejoiced. There was hope we might outlast the camp. The Germans became nervous and impatient with us, increasing our peril daily. Crematoriums were active twenty-four hours a day. More and more shipments of Jews were arriving now from Hungary and Rumania. We were flooded with surplus food. We could tell from the kind of food we were getting where the new arrivals came from.

I befriended a young German prisoner who claimed he turned himself in as a Jew rather than go to the Eastern front where death was almost certain. He was working on a plan of escape by tunneling from the abandoned heating plant which stood next to our barracks. It was a short distance from the plant to the outside. He thought the war was coming to an end and the time was right to try to escape before the Nazis decided to kill us.

Agreeing with his logic, I opted to join him. At every opportunity, we worked on the tunnel. The sandy soil was very soft and easy to dig and we were making fair progress. However, one evening a delegation of the senior prisoners approached us and threatened to expose our plan if we persisted. They feared the retaliation of the guards if we succeeded with our plan. I understood their legitimate concern. We had no right to risk their lives in order to try and save ourselves. We abandoned the work on the tunnel.

Death March

Winter was fast approaching and it is customary in Poland to have the first snowfall by November 1. However, I didn't fear this particular winter because I had good warm clothing, a fine pair of boots and plenty to eat. I was nicely rounded and in good physical condition, ready for whatever came.

The news from the outside was disturbing for the Germans as their armies were in retreat on all fronts. We were hearing about the developments on the eastern front. The Russians were advancing and the Polish underground became more active. There were rumors they might storm Auschwitz and free the prisoners. A faint hope glimmered in all of our hearts.

One morning in early December, we were told there would be no work that day. Then in the early afternoon our camp commandant announced we were moving out. He told us to gather all of our belongings, which in reality were pitifully meager, and assemble outside. As the sun began to set, we marched from Siemens camp, never to see it again.

We walked all night. As we approached Auschwitz we were merged with a huge column of prisoners which stretched for miles. From the direction of our march, we realized we were being directed west towards Germany proper. Many couldn't walk as fast as required in the cold and snow-covered roads. With little strength left in the emaciated bodies of the long-time inmates of the concentration camp, many began to slow down. They were urged by the guards to keep up with the rest. Some just didn't have any strength left or the will to go on; they sat by the roadside in the snow. The guards walked up to them yelling and threatening to shoot them if they didn't move. Some did manage to obey; others looked at the guards with begging gestures and pleaded with them to let them stay for a while. In all the cases I witnessed, the guards stepped away a few feet and fired a volley at the sitting prisoners, who fell back into the snow motionless. The guards then rejoined our marching column admonishing us to move on or the same fate would befall any who stopped.

After midnight, I began to tire. My buddies urged me to keep up. We were passing a small town on the border of Poland and Germany. The population was all German, so possibly we were just inside the German border. There was panic in the streets. People were running to and fro, looking very excited and worried. I understood the end was near. The Russians must be close and the local population, seeing the columns of marching concentration camp prisoners passing through their town, realized what was happening.

Although I thought I was in good physical condition, I was not used to long marches. I felt I couldn't walk any further. As we were passing a large house, I looked around and did not see a guard in sight. Slowly, without making sudden moves, I lingered behind and walked through a large open gate leading to the house. I slipped behind one wing and the wall, and stood quietly while the columns of prisoners continued to pass.

Several German civilians passed the open gate but no one noticed me. My heart was pounding loudly. Then I heard soft footsteps and a voice in Polish: "Severin, are you there?" It was two of my buddies who noticed I was missing and tracked me down to the open gate. They tried to persuade me to go with them back to the column. They kept reminding me that we were in Germany and I would be discovered by the Germans and turned over to the SS. After listening to their reasoning awhile, I decided to go back into the column. I continued my painful march, with each step a supreme effort. At dawn, we reached a small, empty labor camp. With my friends physically helping me, we rushed into one of the buildings. The familiar wooden triple box beds were already full, but we found a spot on the floor where I fell nearly unconscious. I slept most of that day. I was awakened by shouts that soup was being distributed. I then realized I was laying huddled against other bodies on the floor in one tight bundle. This apparently kept us warm during our sleep.

I avidly ate the warm soup. I was again feeling the hunger pains of my early days in the camp and I started scrounging around trying to procure additional food. To my pleasant surprise, I found my friend Bronia. She was a most resolute girl and always had extra food available. We shared half a loaf of camp bread and a piece of sausage. She was in a group of women and men who knew how to obtain special privileges in the camp.

The day went by with many rumors passing among the prisoners: the Germans were leaving and would abandon us there, or the Polish underground was planning an attack on the camp to liberate us, or Russian paratroopers had dropped near us and were advancing on the camp. Unfortunately none of those hopes materialized. In fact, nothing happened as the night approached.

With two of my buddies I returned to the barracks in which I had slept the previous night. However, to my dismay, the building was full of men and women and they had barred the door. I tried to climb through the window but some rough characters beat me off. I was stranded outside with a cold winter night fast approaching and snow had begun to fall. I began wandering from barrack to barrack hoping someone would let me in. No such luck. The situation was getting desperate and I began to feel the chilling cold. Suddenly I thought of Bronia and her friends and found the barrack in which she was staying. I banged my fist on the door calling for Bronia to help me. The door was tightly closed but I heard some voices inside advising against opening it lest the roving mob invade their barracks. I heard Bronia pleading with them on my behalf. I called to her that I was alone at the door and that all she had to do was crack it open and I would slip in. Several men walked to the door and, while holding it slightly ajar, peered outside to make sure I was telling the truth. I was alone as most of my friends had abandoned any hope of finding shelter and had huddled together in the snow to keep warm. "Come in," Bronia whispered from behind the men guarding the door. I slipped in quickly, nearly half frozen. She found a spot on the floor and sat down. I cuddled next to her, resting my head on her lap. She rubbed my body until I felt pleasant warmth overtaking me. Thus, I fell asleep in Bronia's arms, totally exhausted but happy to have survived another day.

In the morning there was some food passed around and I ate, regaining my composure. From outside we heard loud voices of command: "All out! We are marching on! Quick! Form the lines!" I bid a hasty goodbye to Bronia and thanked her for saving my life. Indeed she had, for as I walked outside in the cold but sunny day, I saw many frozen bodies in the snow. These were the men who couldn't find shelter last night.

Columns were being formed outside the barracks. Men were again separated from the women and they marched us off towards a town which was visible in the distance. We walked for about half a day. At noon, we entered the town, which was completely deserted but for a few German patrols.

We entered a large railroad station and were told to wait. Soon a long train pulled in with mostly open gondolas. We were ordered aboard and were herded so tightly that there was only standing room. The sides were high and we couldn't see outside. The train was finally loaded and as it began to slowly pull out we heard the crack of rifle fire. I struggled to climb to the edge of the wagon to see what was going on. A band of men in civilian clothes was shooting at the German guards, who returned their fire. The men fell back as the train picked up speed. They were the Polish underground units trying to free us. Alas, they didn't succeed.

Snow again began to fall as the long train ride began. Fortunately I was with my friends and we huddled together - hungry, cold and dejected - but at least covered by blankets we took from the camp. The train continued to run. Night fell and we slept on and off. In the morning the train stopped in the middle of a forest. We were told to climb down to relieve ourselves. I climbed down and surveyed the situation. Our train car was one of many, all of which were loaded with pale and shivering prisoners. I climbed back and discovered there was considerably more room in the car. To my sorrow, I realized that a number of inmates had died during the night and some of the dead bodies had been piled on top of each other at one side of the car. Many more were lying motionless on the floor. Some of the prisoners threw some of the bodies off the train so as not to have to continue the journey with the dead. However, the guards ordered the prisoners to retrieve all of the bodies and put them back on the train. We then decided to pile all of the dead bodies to one side in order to make room for the living.

We rode another day and night without stopping. I relieved myself by standing on the buffers of the train car. The next night I spent more comfortably as we now had more room to stretch out on the floor. We sat during the day and lay close to one another at night to keep warm. On the third day, the train started to pass through the Czech Republic. We passed bridges on which people stood tossing food parcels despite the fact that the guards were shooting in the air to scare them off. We continued to pass stations where Czechs were standing, apparently waiting for a local train to take them to work. As our train passed, many would open their satchels and bags and toss whatever food they had to us. Unfortunately, I wasn't lucky this time. There were too many of us and too few of them.

In the evening of the third day, we pulled into the main station of Prague. The train stopped. We were ordered out and the guards lined us up in single file. I could hardly walk, my legs felt like they were made of wood; however, the short walk to the main station platform made me feel alive again. There, to our utter amazement, we were greeted by Czech civilian women standing over cauldrons of hot cocoa. Fortunately, I had my ubiquitous bowl with me. I stretched out my dirty, cold hands holding the metal bowl. A kindly, smiling woman ladled hot cocoa into it. Another smiling woman handed me a white roll. I huddled on the ground devouring the roll and sipping the hot cocoa.

To this day, I emotionally remember this fateful outpouring of human kindness. Apparently, a local charitable group persuaded the authorities to allow them to feed us. I will forever have the highest respect and undying gratitude for their humane gesture. One never knows where one might find unexpected help in the direst of situations.

I was revived and my spirits were lifted. The food and the sight of normal humans gave me a renewed burst of energy and strengthened again my will to live.

At dusk on the fourth day of our fateful trip, the train finally stopped. The center doors of the railroad cars were opened and we walked out onto a high station platform. I looked back at my car; it was more than half full of dead bodies. As I passed other cars I saw the same horror scenes. Every one of the

41

cars was half to three quarters full of dead prisoners lying helter skelter like discarded toys.

We formed marching lines in the usual camp manner and walked into a new, huge concentration camp, Buchenwald, one of the largest camps in Bavaria.

More Camps

In Buchenwald, I had to undergo the same entry procedures as in Auschwitz. They took away all my nice clothes, but I persuaded one attendant to let me keep my boots. Amazingly, most of Siemens commando inmates survived the trip. We were kept together as a group but were housed with other prisoners.

Buchenwald was an old and well-organized camp. It became infamous because the sadistic wife of the commandant had lampshades made of the skin of tattooed prisoners. The worst and deadliest work assignment was the quarry, located near the camp, where many prisoners perished daily because of hard work and dangerous conditions. Fortunately I was never assigned to the quarry detail. Several days after our arrival, the Allies (I think it was British aircraft) bombed a nearby machine tool factory, causing substantial damage to the town. We were awakened at 2:00 a.m. and, without any nourishment, marched to the railroad station, loaded on freight cars and taken to the nearby city of Augsburg. We marched from the station to the damaged part of town where we were separated into groups of twenty. Each group was assigned to a damaged building. Our job was to gather the scattered bricks and stones of the bombed houses. As always, the work progressed at a snail's pace. Very little was done because the guards were scattered and the supervision was lax. This gave me an opportunity to climb on the ruins of the houses to the second, or even third floors, in order to enter in search of food. I was lucky again. In one apartment the kitchen was intact. There was stale bread and jars of marmalade. I stuffed all I could inside my clothing and climbed down to share the trove with my friends. This find was especially providential as we were not given anything to eat all day. For the next several days we were taken back to the bombed city. One day a woman appeared in an opening of the second floor of a partially demolished house, called out to our group, and tossed a bundle of food from her apartment. We ran quickly to inspect the gift. The bundle, wrapped in a white sheet, was full of bread and rolls. What a treat for us! This kindness demonstrated that many German civilians pitied us and, when they knew they would not be detected, tried to assist the prisoners.

In the spring our group was told we were being assigned back to Siemens and would be shipped to one of their plants. On a beautiful April morning the original Siemens commando was mustered out of Buchenwald, loaded in closed cattle cars, and sent north. The trip took several days. I so vividly remember one terrible evening when we were shunted on a side track waiting for other trains to pass. Two guards were standing in front of our car, speaking loudly enough for me to hear, and one of them said: "The Jew Roosevelt died; let's hope the war will come to an end now." My heart stopped a beat! President Roosevelt passed away! What will happen to us? Will the Americans continue to fight? Who will save us? This was truly a most dark moment during my imprisonment. Hope was all we had left and it seemed dashed by the sudden death of the most illustrious of American presidents. The terrible news ran throughout the train. There were many sobs, and prayers were said in many languages since we were a mixed group of Europeans.

Finally the train stopped and the doors were opened. The sign on the station read: Berlin - Siemensstadt. We were assigned to the main Siemens plant. We marched to a camp in the middle of a residential part of town. The camp was small but considerably better than the concentration camps of the past. There were several rows of small barracks with the ubiquitous wooden three-tier berths, but everything was clean and well kept.

The next day Siemens' civilian employees came to the camp and told us we would be working on the second shift. We were allowed to rest all day. At 4:00 p.m. we were marched through a residential street lined on both sides with large apartment buildings dating to the beginning of the century. The typical red brick structures were built in the heavy and solid German style. It gave me great pleasure to be walking in this elegant and western town. I felt like I was back in civilization again, it was so different from the barbaric life in the camps. The daily walk back and forth to the plant was full of wonderment of the western European life which I had almost forgotten existed. We always marched in the middle of the street. I could look left and right to see well-dressed people, shops, and the daily bustle of life, although somewhat subdued due to the fact that the war was on and there was the prevailing blackout. At the beginning of the month of May, we had daily air raids. During the day it was the American bombers and at night the British. We could nearly tell the exact hour by the sirens sounding the alarm. During the day we had to leave our barracks and climb down to the bomb shelters, which were just open trenches between the barracks. The guards occupied peripheral trenches. Those shelters were well camouflaged with low turrets so they could watch us during the air raids. During our second shifts, we were ordered by our civilian bosses to close all tool boxes and prepare for the air raid, which sounded punctually at 11:45 p.m. every single night. We would all walk down to the cellar where strong bomb-proof shelters were erected for the safety of the Siemens workers. This became a regular routine for all of us.

Then, one night at the end of May, Siemens was hit by heavy bombing. The entire shelter shook and heaved. The powerful force of the exploding bombs seemed to lift and shift the entire bomb shelter. It was very frightening. We found ourselves on the receiving side of the British night bombing. When the all clear sounded, we climbed out to an unbelievable sight - the plant was completely destroyed. There remained a pile of rubble of what was once a large plant. It was nearly 3:00 a.m. before we reached our camp. On the way, we saw the devastation the bombing raid had caused in the town. Buildings were burning like infernos. People were running to and fro. Women were weeping, lamenting and wringing their hands in despair, looking at their houses and their belongings going up in smoke. All I could think was: Hallelujah!! The German population had begun to feel the cruelty of war. They were on the receiving end this time.

The next day at noon the American bombers arrived over our camp. They were dropping bombs all around us but not a single bomb fell on our prison camp. I was amazed at what I thought was their exceptionally good aim. Later in the afternoon another wave of American planes arrived, but this time the planes were smaller. They began strafing our camp. We all ran to our shelters, but since they were open trenches we could easily see the low-flying planes. The guards were now returning the fire from their observation towers. Several bombs fell. We all hugged the ground which shook violently. When the all clear sounded, and we climbed out of the shelters, we saw what havoc they had wrought. The entire camp was in flames. The outer trenches occupied by the guards were in shambles. All observation turrets were badly damaged. There were many dead German guards and many badly wounded calling for help. This was a horrible scene of carnage which resulted from the unbelievable aim of the American airmen. By a true miracle, no prisoners were killed or even wounded, with the exception of one man who panicked and jumped out of the trenches and was hit by one of the exploding bombs.

The surviving guards rounded us up and marched us off to a metro station. The train left the station but had to stop at the next one. Another air raid was in progress. The underground stations were used as air raid shelters, and we sat a long time in the train looking at the civilian and military population huddled on the platform. There was a young girl, maybe high school age, sitting on a suitcase and next to her sat a young German soldier. They huddled together, embracing and kissing one another. I was riveted to this scene, which I somehow never forgot. There in the middle of war, I watched life continuing despite all of the uncertainty which surrounded them. Life does go on no matter what is happening around you. This bittersweet tableau left a deep impression on me.

Eventually the train pulled out, and after a while the subway became an elevated train and I could see plainly many parts of Berlin. It was a devastated city with piles of rubble to be seen everywhere. Many of the streets were free of the rubble, but instead of houses, there were neat piles of stones orderly arranged in the German fashion.

Finally we arrived at our destination. I could not believe my eyes when we walked through the gates marked Sachsenhausen. Here I was, finally in the camp where my father had wanted me to be. It was a very large camp built in much better style than Auschwitz. The camp consisted of various sections: men's camp, women's, and political prisoners' camp. I was admitted to the main and also largest section, namely the men's camp. After the evening meal we were treated every day to the official radio broadcast of the German forces. We listened attentively, trying to get to the truth of the situation. Whenever the radio announced that the army occupied new and more advantageous positions, we understood they actually were in full retreat.

The first thing I did upon my arrival was to look for my father and uncle. Unfortunately, I was told I was about a month too late. The Germans closed the secret commando and moved all inmates and the equipment elsewhere. At least I could look at the spot where my family had stayed until a short while before my arrival. The special camp stood empty like a ghost town. Later, my father told me his unbelievable story, which I have since seen documented in various books. He and my uncle were moved to southern Bavaria near the Swiss border.

There, surrounded by breathtaking scenery, they attempted to restart the operation at an abandoned factory where nothing worked anymore. The camp administrators were preparing for a sudden departure since they realized the war was coming to an end. The American 42nd Rainbow Division under the command of General Clark was advancing from the south along the Swiss border. One beautiful spring morning the camp commandant, who had taken a liking to my father, called him into his office. He informed him he was departing, along with all the officers and the SS guards, leaving the prisoners under the charge of ordinary army units. Father's office was next to the commandant's so he could see when he began loading several suitcases of falsified British five-pound notes. There were other currencies in the safe which the commandant emptied as well. A staff car pulled up in front of the office and all the suitcases were loaded in the trunk. The commandant came over to my father, shook his hand, and after wishing him good luck departed toward the Swiss border. Soon there was a change of guards, the SS left and a group of older-looking soldiers took over. The new army officer in charge asked my father what he was doing in the office so close to his. After my father properly explained, he ordered him to stay on and continue his work. However, what my father was actually doing was copying the serial numbers the Germans had printed on the forged five-pound notes. Risking his life, he placed the sheets with serial numbers under his clothes, assuming the Allies would want to know the numbers of the false currencies, especially the ones in circulation. He was assisted by a fellow prisoner named Glass who was his co-worker in the serial-number record-keeping office.

Days passed and the prisoners were idling their time anxiously awaiting developments, which were unfolding very quickly. Then one day the army officers gathered all the prisoners and announced the American army was in the next village. One of the German soldiers walked up to the gate, opened it and slowly withdrew. My father, my uncle and Mr. Glass didn't need another hint. Cautiously they moved toward the open gate and once outside began to run. Others followed quickly.

His first inclination was to go in the direction of the advancing Americans. They walked for several hours. There was very little traffic and no one bothered them, despite the fact they were in prison garb. Finally they reached a quaint village. They refreshed themselves drinking water from a communal fountain in the center of the village. There was virtually no one around. It was eerily quiet as they sat resting on a bench. Suddenly they heard the rumble of approaching vehicles, which quickly pulled into the village square and stopped just in front of the bench where they were sitting. My father jumped to his feet, his heart pounding, and stared in near disbelief. These dusty, dirty, disheveled men in green uniforms, but with rounded helmets so different from the ones he was used to seeing, were the spearhead of the advancing armored division. My father and Mr. Glass ran to the astounded soldiers, yelling: "Americans! Americans! Thank God these are Americans!"

My father's English at that time was rather sketchy, being self-taught during the war. He started explaining to one of the soldiers that he had important information for the Allies. The GI called for his superior, to whom my father and Mr. Glass tried to explain what interesting information they had. The officer listened attentively and asked them to wait while he radioed headquarters. He then returned and asked them to remain as someone would come

48

to talk to them. In the meantime, he ordered two "K" rations for my father and his companions. A few hours went by. Eventually a jeep pulled up in front of their bench and two men from CIC walked up to talk to my father. After listening to his story, they asked him and Mr. Glass to accompany them to headquarters.

Thus began the long odyssey of my father and Mr. Glass. They were passed from one office to another and eventually incarcerated by the American forces. No one really believed them until my father divulged the location of the lake where the Nazis dumped the printed banknotes. Divers were sent to verify his story and came up with cases full of British five-pound notes. Somehow, though, the allied authorities weren't sure of my dad's involvement and locked him up in Spandau prison, where later all the Nazi criminals were tried.

Fortunately the story had a quasi-happy ending. After a few frustrating and uneasy days, two officers came to their cell and apologized. They thanked my father profusely for the information he provided and told both they were free to go. My dad and his friend expected a reward for risking their lives, but they were happy to be free at last, and left without saying a word. I am not sure that they didn't murmur a few choice words while leaving the prison, but I leave that to the readers' imagination.

Meanwhile, I was still in the hands of the Germans, not knowing what would happen next. During the few days in Sachsenhausen I did the usual menial and senseless work which I had encountered before, namely digging long trenches for no purpose whatsoever. The Germans thought it was necessary for us to work, but most of the time there was no need for the work we performed. I went with others to work every morning. As we passed the main gate of the camp there were always some men and women standing facing the building in front. They were all painted with black paint and wearing large signs: "I am a criminal." These were German nationals caught in ration coupon transgressions. Often, upon our return, we found them either still standing or lying on the ground. The following day there would be another batch of these unfortunate people standing at the gate. I was told the firing squad finished each contingent at dusk.

One evening there was an unusual turmoil in all the camps. At night someone had cut the wires separating the camps, and prisoners were moving everywhere. I slept very fitfully that night, which turned out to be my last night in the camp. In the morning there was no food distribution. Through the loudspeaker system we were ordered to assemble at the main gate, take all our belongings and be prepared to march out. Some suggested we ought to hide in one of the barracks. I considered that option and walked into one of the empty buildings. On the ground floor I found two young women hiding under a box stall. They were frightened and looked at me apprehensively. I told them not to be afraid, that I, too, was looking to hide. After a while I decided that it was not a good idea to hide inside a prison camp. I preferred to take my chances on the outside.

I joined my friends near the main gate, and soon after we were marched outside the camp. It was a beautiful spring day. The sun was shining and it was pleasantly warm. I noticed we were marching in a northerly direction. Along the way there were signs of the German defeat. Often along the road I would notice pieces of military clothing dumped by apparently disbanding German troops. Later in the march I saw many rifles thrown in the ditches. At the end of the first day some of the guards told us they were staying behind to defend our rear and would join us later. We never saw them again. There were fewer guards now and we were treated a lot better than during the death march from Auschwitz.

The first night we spent in a forest, huddled together to keep warm. Fortunately I had taken my bed blanket and so did many others. We could wrap ourselves in them and kept relatively comfortable all night. In the morning there was the usual hot herbal tea and on that alone we were to march all day. Obviously, I was getting hungry. My buddies were more resourceful than I, and during their last hour at the camp they had managed to scrounge a few potatoes and other edible roots, which were the integral parts of our daily soups. I had a metal drinking cup which we perforated on the sides. We placed twigs of wood into the cup and ignited them. While marching, I swung the cup on several strings to keep the fire burning. When it was nice and hot, we sliced potatoes or whatever was available and cooked them while marching.

What kept us going was the overwhelming appearance of the agony of the German war machine. We passed through well kept, prosperous villages with the inhabitants in a state of panic. What a satisfying picture that made! It was early spring and the country looked even more beautiful than usual. My spirits soared, especially as the signs of the German defeat became more and more apparent. Every day there were several air raid alerts. When the roar of the planes was near, the guards ordered us to stop in the middle of the road as they sought shelter in the ditches alongside. The planes would fly very low over us, and seeing that we were prisoners would then veer off. When the all clear sounded, we resumed our march.

The story was very different at dusk when we left the road to spend the night in the forest. We could hear the strafing planes hitting whatever was moving on the road. When we resumed the march in the morning, there were signs of their action: burned-out vehicles, dead people, and most importantly, dead horses. We pounced on their carcasses, often still warm, and tore off a piece of flesh which we cooked in our portable, makeshift ovens, or we waited until night to cook the meat over the fires. This is how I survived the long march.

One evening before we were ordered off the road, I noticed several supply trucks with large red crosses marked on all sides. By the trucks stood several uniformed men who didn't appear to be German. As I approached them I noticed the inscription on their uniforms: "CANADA." An unbelievable thing had happened. The International Red Cross was sending food supplies to the starving prisoners. These were the first large-size food ration packages I ever saw. The German guards took the cigarettes, chocolate and other delicacies, then the rest of the contents of the packages was distributed among us. Each person received one item. It was my luck to get a can of powdered milk. I quickly opened it and started licking the powder, which of course didn't go down very well. I turned to my buddy who got a can of Canadian butter. Luckily, other friends got biscuits and Spam. So we exchanged and combined our gifts so that everyone had something good to eat. We made hot milk with my powder which everyone greatly enjoyed.

The next two days went uneventfully. It was getting colder and a strong wind was blowing from the north. We were on the outskirts of Rostock in Mecklenburg, only a few miles from the North Sea. That night we were herded into a large abandoned quarry. The guards were posted on the rim with machine guns pointed in our direction. We were not allowed fires that night. In the usual manner, we laid our blankets on the ground and lay next to one another in groups of six or seven, using the remaining blankets to cover our bodies in order to protect ourselves from the cold and wet wind.

For some reason I slept fitfully, waking up several times. The cold dawn finally arrived. I was the first one up from my group. I noticed an unusual commotion and agitation among the other prisoners. I asked what was wrong. Someone pointed to the rim above us. The guards were gone! I couldn't believe my eyes. I thought I was still asleep and this must be a dream. I rubbed my eyes, I pinched myself. No! It was true. The guards were gone - we were free!

Most of my friends were up by this time. We looked at one another in sheer disbelief. What do we do now? Someone suggested we should sit down and discuss it as a group. We sat down and heard a wild, guttural yell of joy coming from the nearby group. We all chimed in. I don't know how long we sat and yelled aimlessly, venting our frustration.

I nudged my buddy and said, "Let's get out of here before the Germans change their minds." The rest preferred to stay and wait to see what happened. We climbed out of the quarry and over a steep embankment at the rim. There were several guards nearby. We walked up to them and asked what was going on. They pointed to the west saying the Americans were very close and should be there sometime that day. I didn't wait for this to happen. My buddy and I took off across the fields to the nearest farmhouse. We timidly approached the buildings. There was a sizable group of people - Germans and prisoners - standing in the farm yard. Someone was handing out cups of milk and there were slices of bread on the table. We drank and ate our fill, thanked the hosts and headed in a western direction.

We walked a good part of the day. About noon we were crossing some woods when we encountered several prisoners coming out between the trees and motioning for us to join them. We followed their direction and came upon a large army kitchen. The bivouac must have been abandoned recently because the food was still warm. I opened one hot cauldron - it was full of heavenly smelling pea soup. My all-time favorite. Well, you can imagine our happiness. I ate, and ate, and ate, until I couldn't swallow any more. We scrounged around and found a large container with whole chickens. We loaded ourselves with this trove and marched off. In the evening we stopped at a farmhouse and asked if we could spend the night in the barn. Granted permission, we slept, for the first time free, and very happy! In the morning we cooked our chicken in the farmyard, tidied up and thanked the landlady for her hospitality. She asked if we would stay because she was afraid of the Russian soldiers who she heard were raping all the women they came in contact with. We told her we could not stay as we wanted to reach the American lines. We continued walking most of the day. In the early afternoon, we noticed that the road was nearly empty. We had passed several German units stationed alongside the road. They didn't seem to notice us. Sometime later, while looking ahead, I noticed tanks straddling the road. As we approached them, fearing the worst, I was straining my eyes to ascertain whose tanks they were. A large group of POWs caught up with us. They still had German guards around them. The prisoners were Allies, laughing and talking loudly as they passed. We decided to follow them. Soon I could easily see the large white five-pointed star painted on the tanks. An armed American soldier was standing in front of them, carefully surveying the approaching groups. We stopped for a moment to see what would happen to the POWs; they passed between the tanks. The German guards removed their guns and handed them to several GI's who took them into custody.

We approached next. The American soldier looked at us for a moment and motioned for us to come closer. When we approached, he pointed to an area behind the tanks. He didn't say a word and none was necessary. In the blink of an eye we were on the other side of the barrier. We were saved!

That same evening we were taken in trucks to a large German military camp which was filling up with recently freed prisoners. It was there that I discovered the ultimate goal of our march. The Germans were planning to ship us to Norway, where we were to build defense trenches for the remnants of the German army. Fortunately my group was not in the forefront. The first wave of marchers reached the sea and was jam-packed into freighters which then left the harbor for the open sea. Allied planes circled the armada ordering the ships to return to port. The Germans refused. The planes then torpedoed the boats, drowning most aboard. There were very few survivors. For months the bodies of the drowned prisoners washed up on the shore. I was miraculously spared! The year was 1945.

Photographs

Severin Fayerman - approximately 3 years old

Mother Felicia, favorite uncle Simon, and Severin at
a Baltic Sea resort, July 1934

Aunt Regina (apparently killed by the Russians), Severin,
and his mother Felicia, Winter 1938

Severin's military government pass issued to
former concentration camp prisoners

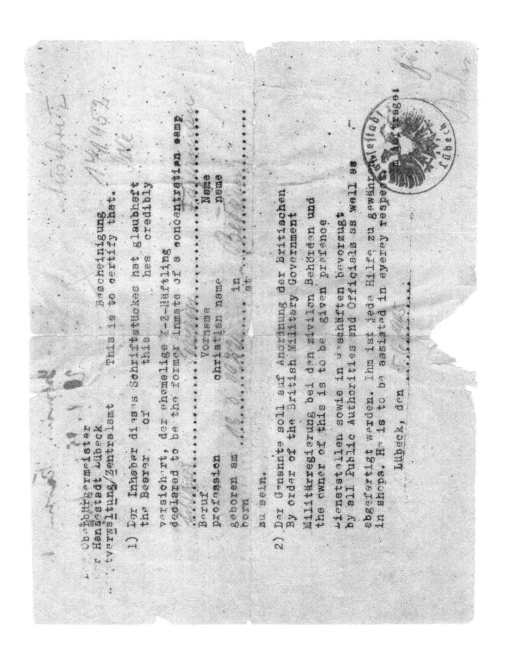

Severin's first identification document, issued by the
Buergermeister (mayor) of Luebeck, Germany

Severin's father Henry, mother Felicia, and uncle Simon
in Austria on a mountain hike

Severin Fayerman in his UNRRA uniform
before leaving for America

Severin's identification paper while working for UNRRA

NAME: SEWERYN FAJERMAN

PERMANENT ADDRESS: 13 Markus Sittikus, Salzburg, Austria

NATIONALITY : Polish

SIGNATURE OF BEARER:

IDENTIFYING INFORMATION

AGE 23   WEIGHT 136 lbs
HEIGHT 1 m. 72
COLOR OF HAIR   Brown
COLOR OF EYES   Blue

NEAREST RELATIVE (to be notified in case of accident or illness): Mrs. Felicia Fajerman (Mother)

13 Markus Sittikus

Salzburg, Austria

UNRRA
AUSTRIAN OPERATION

NAME: SEWERYN FAJERMAN
POSITION: Clerk
DATE ISSUED: 29 October 1945
SIGNATURE OF ISSUING OFFICER: R. S. STOWELL
Personnel Officer

CERTIFICATE OF IDENTITY

No. 09040

"In memory of our meeting again at Salzburg"
September 1945

Severin on the way from Salzburg, Austria to Hamburg, Germany
and the embarkation for the voyage to the United States

Severin's father, Henry, aboard the transport ship
Marine Perch while sailing to America

Severin at the company's Newark, NJ
office at 5 Kirk Place

The family sightseeing in New York Harbor while
getting acquainted with their new homeland

Marjorie and Severin in front of parents' house
in West Orange, NJ, 1950

Marjorie and Severin on their first business trip
to London, England in 1954

Free At Last!

The temporary camp in which I found myself was a former German U-Boat school. It was a large and modern installation consisting of several buildings ideally suited for housing freed prisoners of various forced labor and concentration camps. The installation was located on the edge of a small seaside town in Schleswick-Holstein. We were allowed to leave the premises during the day and wander around the town.

For the first few days I was in a total state of shock. I had to get used to the fact that I was actually free and had survived the war. I needed peace and time to return to a normal life. When I regained my strength, my first thought was to try to find my parents, which would not be an easy task as there was no communication available. We were virtually cut off from the outside world. There was a state of chaos everywhere and a curfew was strictly observed. I approached the camp director and asked if he had any employment for me. He was an American army officer and a very nice person. He was pleasantly surprised to find an English speaking individual who was fluent in several languages. He hired me to do some general office duties but mainly I was an interpreter for the many different nationalities seeking assistance. I soon discovered that the main function of the camp was to repatriate all prisoners. Through the military channels, trucks and trains were being sent to bring back various nationals. Soon trucks arrived from France, Belgium, and Holland, gathering their nationals for return to their respective countries. My French friends from Siemens invited me to come with them. I decided against it since I wanted, at all cost, to start looking for my family as soon as possible.

The Russians sent trains and a few Communist party agents to screen their nationals. They told me I could go along with them and they would drop me

67

off in Poland on their way to Russia. I didn't like the party people and, having witnessed a few unpleasant episodes, I decided not to trust them. Poland sent for no one; we were told to make our way back on foot. I then discovered there was a new camp being formed in a nearby town for those who could not return to their homeland due to political situations in their respective countries. I opted to go to this camp. This was my first experience with UNRRA, (United Nations Relief and Rehabilitation Administration), an arm of the UN. The new camp consisted of several multi-story buildings in which lived men and women freed from camps in Germany. Most of the inmates were from Eastern Europe.

As soon as I arrived at the UNRRA camp, I applied for work in the camp administration. With a letter of recommendation from my American officer friend, I was hired at once. I acted as an interpreter and performed various office duties. I learned that there were many such camps throughout Germany. There was a liaison officer who visited nearby camps on a regular basis and I persuaded him to let me go with him on his scheduled visits.

In every camp there was a list of inmates posted on the bulletin board. I scanned them carefully to see if there were any familiar names. We stayed long enough in each camp to allow me to circulate and look for people from my home town in the hope that they may have heard of anyone from my family who survived the war. I did meet a number of people from my town and from various camps in which I had been imprisoned. There were many happy moments, particularly when I found my friend Bronia from Siemens, who had been so good to me. I persuaded the UNRRA liaison officer to leave me in the camp with my friend for a few days. He agreed and promised to pick me up on the way back to my camp up north. The camp where Bronia stayed was for girls only, but male members of the girls' families were allowed to stay if no one objected. Bronia said I was her cousin and that she wanted to be with me. I spent a few days in heaven, but, all good things must come to an end and I returned to my camp with the liaison officer.

Upon my return, I found that a new procedure was being introduced at the camp. Namely, the liaison officer was to pick up a list of inmates of camps throughout Germany and distribute them as a means of getting scattered families together. I was given the job of reviewing each list and posting it on the bulletin board.

One beautiful day there arrived a stack of lists and on one of them was the name of Simon Fayerman, my uncle, who had been taken with my father to Sachsenhausen. You can imagine my joy. I was absolutely beside myself. I promptly approached our camp director and explained the situation and requested permission to go to the camp where, apparently, my uncle was staying. My burning question was, however, where was my father? Why wasn't his name on the list? After all, they were together in the same camp during the war.

Well anyway, I thought, at least I was not alone. I had my favorite uncle somewhere in Germany, most probably wondering if I, too, had survived. The camp director gave me a letter of recommendation requesting all authorities to assist me. I packed my meager belongings in a bundle and stepped outside the camp, with no money, no resources, and no definite plan of action. The camp was on a main route frequented by U.S. army trucks. As one approached, I lifted my thumb and the truck stopped. A friendly voice called to me in English, asking where I was going. I told him of my destination, which was in Bavaria. The soldier replied, "Hop in; I am going in the same direction."

On the way we became friends. He shared his K rations with me and I was happily on my way to my uncle. Although the truck would have taken me very close to my destination, it was crossing the Russian zone of occupation and the driver told me the Russians would not let me pass and would surely detain me. So late that afternoon, shortly before entering the Russian zone, I left the truck. I found a German Travelers Aid Station where they gave me an evening meal and a mattress to sleep on. In the morning, a cup of coffee, and a good luck send-off, left me outside the building on a busy street. The passing trucks would stop to pick up civilians and I found a truck going in the direction of the Bavarian town where I expected to find my uncle.

However, I briefly interrupted my search to stop at Bergen-Belsen Camp where I had left Bronia. She was happy to see me and excitedly informed me that she had just received information that her cousin was in a small town near Munich. I offered to take her there. After much difficulty, we finally found him comfortably established, living with a nice German family. I left Bronia with her cousin, promising to return after I found my parents.

When mail service was restored, I wrote to her in care of the German family. I eventually discovered that she had left with the intention of returning to Poland. Sadly, I completely lost track of this resourceful, wonderful girl whose help several times was instrumental in my survival.

Resuming my search, many truck and train rides later I arrived at my destination and found the camp I was looking for. It was nearly dark when I finally located the director of the camp and asked for my uncle. They checked the list and indeed found the name of Simon Fayerman but could not locate him. He simply wasn't there and no one had seen or heard of him. I asked how this was possible. Simple, I was told. Many people pass through the camp and they register the names of people they know survived the camps. So, although disappointed, at least I knew my uncle was alive.

The camp was full so I spent an uncomfortable night sleeping on the floor. In the morning, as I sat on the floor of a busy corridor, a thought suddenly struck me. I remembered my father's words as we huddled in the cold train on the way to Auschwitz: "If we survive, let's all reunite in Salzburg."

Consequently, I picked up my bundle and set out on my way to Austria via the usual, haphazard means of transportation. A long odyssey began of many stops and many camps. I decided however to arrive in Salzburg in style. I procured a modest suitcase, a suit of clothes and extra suit material. All of this was made possible through various German charitable organizations which were being established to clothe and rehabilitate the former prisoners of various camps, most of whom were still in the striped pajamas they had received in their respective camps. There was just one gift per person, but using my ingenuity, I posed as different people and doubled or tripled the gifts. Now I had some money and had accumulated a bit of worldly goods.

One sunny afternoon, I arrived at a town near the Austrian border. I was traveling the usual open truck method with several other Germans. The truck stopped to discharge someone and refuel. Suddenly, I heard my name called from the street. It was my neighbor from Bendzin, a girl I knew very well and who was a good friend of the family. I jumped from the truck and ran to greet her. After many hugs and kisses, she exclaimed: "Severin, do you know your parents and Uncle Simon are in Salzburg looking for you?" I couldn't believe what I heard. But she assured me it was true and tears of joy at giving me this wonderful news flooded her round, red cheeks. I hugged her and inquired about her family. They were all dead, she said, now crying vehemently.

The truck driver blew the horn and called for me to get back on. I kissed her for the last time and ran to catch the slowly moving truck. I waved and waved until I lost sight of her. I stood in the truck - as it picked up speed, with the wind blowing in my face - stunned. It was really true. My family was alive and well. What amazing good luck!

The truck stopped in a small town on the border of Austria and I left it walking directly to the point of crossing. The border check point was guarded by American sentries. I asked permission to cross but was instead directed to the officer in charge. First, I had to present my credentials. Then the officer asked me if I was an Austrian subject. I told him I was not. Then he told me I could not cross as only Austrians were allowed to enter their country. My pleas and protestations had no effect. I simply was not allowed to enter Austria and that was final.

I was very disappointed and distressed as I retraced my steps from the border crossing point. A little way up the road I found a large farm and headed toward the main house. I asked permission to spend the night in the barn. The owner was a kind man and told me there was room in the bunk house. He also invited me to join them for the evening meal. During the dinner conversation, I told him of my problem with crossing the border to Austria. He listened attentively and then said: "Don't worry, they are kind Americans and will not bother you tomorrow. I will take you across the border by a small path which we all knowingly use when we want to go to Salzburg."

Indeed, the next morning the farmer woke me early and after a fine breakfast we left the house and took the road back to the check point. I wondered how we were going to deal with the sentries. A few hundred feet from the check point, the farmer led me to a narrow path which circumvented the check point at a close distance. Shortly, the path led back to the highway on the other side of the check point. "You are in Austria now," said the farmer.

"Follow the road for about a mile; you will come to a farmhouse by the road. Stop there and ask for Herr Keller and tell him I sent you. He will take you in his truck to Salzburg." I thanked the farmer profusely and took to the completely empty road. Soon I came to the house in which Mr. Keller resided. He was a nice person and very helpful. I again told my story and asked his advice as to how I could find my parents. Mr. Keller said it would be best to go to the organization in town established to help people in my position. He took me to the city of Salzburg and deposited me in front of the office of an aid society for former prisoners of war. The office was located on the second floor of the municipal building. I knocked on the door and walked into a large room with a desk at the window. I introduced myself to the gentleman seated behind the desk and asked if he knew where my parents lived. The man looked at me for a while and a large smile crossed his face. He slowly rose from his chair, walked around the desk and stood in front of me. Then he said the most wonderful words, "You are the first person to whom I can say your father and mother are here in Salzburg together with your Uncle Simon. I will take you to them at once." We climbed in his car and drove out of the city center to a nice residential street. He suddenly stopped the car near a garden wall and said, "Let me go first and see your parents. The shock of the news may be too much for your mother. Your parents come to my office every day to ask if we have any news of you." He then left me and walked into a nearby house. At the first floor was a woman in the window. It was my mother! I couldn't restrain myself any longer and I stepped out of the car. Suddenly, I heard a loud shriek: "My baby, my baby, I see Severin." There was an unbelievable and forever unforgettable scene when my family ran out of the house to greet me. Unquestionably, this was the happiest moment in my life!

My mother later told me some force drew her to the window that morning when the car stopped near the house; somehow she knew I was in it. As soon as she saw the man from the aid office walking up to the house, she was then certain I was in the car.

All day we told each other about the experiences during our separation. We commemorated that day by signing a black and white drawing of a scene of Salzburg, which I still have in my possession. I proudly showed my parents what I had accumulated since the end of the war. It was all contained in a small suitcase which I carried with me through the entire trip. It wasn't much but I wanted to show them how I had managed for myself.

We enjoyed several weeks of our reunion but more often the talk turned to the subject of what we were going to do with our lives now that we were liberated. My parents had returned to Bendzin to find their factory nationalized by the new Polish government. My father was offered a job in his own factory but his friends advised him to leave the country as the previous owners of business establishments were not welcome. There were concerns that he might be prosecuted for trumped-up charges just to get rid of him.

My dad seriously considered their advice and decided to make a trip to the capital in Warsaw. He wanted to investigate the present climate and hear from higher authorities if the situation was temporary or permanent. He was told that under the new government constitution no private ownership was allowed for businesses with more than ten employees. After weighing this distressing news, he decided it would be best to emigrate. One dark night he and my mother packed two suitcases each and crossed the border to Czechoslovakia and continued on to Austria. My Uncle Simon, all this time, was in Salzburg waiting for their return.

It was during these talks that we decided we would not stay in Austria but try to emigrate to America, Canada, Australia or New Zealand. We hoped we could find a way to America through the Occupation Forces in Austria, and that is eventually what happened. I proposed to get a job with the Americans hoping we could somehow find an opening to leave Europe. I went to UNRRA with my letter of recommendation. Their headquarters were located in Salzburg. I was told politely that there was no work for me in the office and the only opening they had was a job as a night watchman. The interviewer thought I would not want to do that; however, I jumped at the opportunity. A job is a job, I thought, and at least I would be employed by the Americans.

The work was very easy. I reported at 5:00 pm. and stayed until midnight. My duties consisted of waiting for a telephone call from any UNRRA official traveling to Salzburg and direct him to one of their billets. Also, I was to assist the American GI's who arrived every evening at 6:00 p.m. with a crew of Austrian civilians to clean the offices. After a few weeks, I returned to the office during the day and asked if they had anything additional for me to do as I was bored doing so little. This apparently impressed the officer in charge as a few days later he left a note for me to see him the following day. I was pleasantly surprised when I was offered a job as a mail registrar but was told that first I had to find a replacement for the night watchman's job.

"No problem," I said. The following day I had a charming lady present herself as an applicant for my job. My family had met her in Salzburg and they became friends. Her husband had escaped to America before the war and she was waiting with her children for the opportunity to join him there. She spoke better English than I in addition to several other European languages. Before the war, her family was one of the richest in Poland. The personnel director was more than a little surprised to find such a fine women applying for a night watchman's job but he was so impressed by Mrs. Orski that he couldn't say no. The deal was done! I was on a day job in the UNRRA office and had reached the first step to our goal.

My dad went to the office of the American Red Cross and got a job with them. We were both keeping our eyes and ears open for any news of an opportunity to emigrate to the USA.

In the fall of 1945, a new UNRRA mission was opened in Vienna to help the local population return to normal life. Vienna was at that time in the Soviet zone of occupation but the city proper was administered by the US forces and the three Allies: Britain, France and Russia. I was asked if I wanted to go there and was offered a job as a registrar with officer's privileges. I jumped at the offer. I was given a British uniform because as a Pole I belonged to the Polish contingent of the British army. How proud I was to wear it! Immediately after my mother sewed the UNRRA red and white insignia on the shoulders of the uniform, I paraded in the streets reveling in (what I believed to be) the admiring looks of the population. Indeed, I was proud of my new uniform. My parents were not happy to see me leave them but understood it was an opportunity for me to advance in our quest for a better life.

The UNRRA staff was housed in a beautiful hotel near the center of town. I had my own room and received three meals a day in the restaurant. The hotel and our offices were located in the American zone. My work was interesting; I made many new friends and loved every minute of my new life in Vienna. The only thing missing was a girlfriend. After dinner I would walk the streets looking for a likely candidate. One evening, I spotted a nice-looking lady holding a large size shopping bag. I approached her and asked directions to the hotel where I was staying. She said she was going in the same direction and could show me the way. I offered to carry her bag and she hesitantly allowed me to take it. Thus began a long relationship which continued until my departure from Vienna. She was a war widow and readily accepted my companionship. The strange part of our meeting, I later learned, was that although she was employed in a municipal office, she was earning extra money by doing a little black marketing after work. That particular evening when I approached her for the first time, she was waiting to meet with her supplier of black market goods. She initially thought I was a military policeman and was relieved when she realized I was only clumsily trying to pick her up. She led me away from the spot where she was expecting her contact fearing exposure of her activity. Thus, unaware that I was carrying contraband goods, I escorted my new friend to her apartment.

Later on, she helped me sell my PX goods. I was entitled to officer's rations which were very generous, especially in the quantity of cigarettes and liquor. These goods were very much in demand in post war Vienna. This was part of the financial arrangement I made with UNRRA. As a civilian, I was paid in script money (a currency printed by the US forces to pay local civilians for their services.) This script money could be exchanged for Austrian shillings at a bank. Since I needed little money to live on, I asked our finance officer to save my pay until the time I was able to go to the United States. In the meantime, I lived royally on the revenue I received from the PX goods I sold through my friend. Life for me was peaches and cream. I went to excellent concerts and plays and enjoyed the sophisticated life which had quickly returned to post war Vienna. I took advantage of every opportunity afforded me.

Then one day a middle-aged officer named Miss Aleta Brownlee arrived at the mission. She was a child welfare specialist. Her endeavor was to find children from countries occupied by Germany during the war who had been separated from their parents and given to various German farm families to rear as their own. There was an urgent appeal from the International Red Cross to help reunite them with their parents, who were frantically searching for their stolen children.

Miss Brownlee was looking for an interpreter. I applied immediately and after a short interview was hired for the job. We traveled throughout all three zones of occupation looking for children who were given to Austrian farmers to rear as their own. It was a long and strenuous search but we succeeded in finding several children who were turned over to the International Red Cross for return to their respective countries. We were delighted when we found the children, hoping they, in turn, would be reunited with their parents. I knew how wonderful that would feel.

After each trip of a week to ten days, Miss Brownlee and I would return to Vienna. During one of these rounds, I discovered that UNRRA was arranging for displaced persons to be sent to America. President Truman had directed the Immigration Department to allow as many displaced Europeans to come to the USA as quotas would allow. During the war years the immigration from Europe ceased, thus, the quotas were not filled. I was in the first line to apply, together with my father, mother and Uncle Simon. We were all accepted but were told we could not go on the first ship as it was set aside for orphans only. Well, I thought, we waited so long, another few weeks would not matter.

I quit my job at UNRRA, went back to Salzburg and gathered my eager family, happily awaiting the time to leave Austria. We were taken by train from Salzburg to Munich, Germany. There we were processed by the Immigration authorities and sent by train to Hamburg. The train went right up to the docks and stopped at a troop transport ship, "Marine Perch."

Thus began our voyage of ten days on the sea, which would take us to our final destination. During the trip my family worked feverishly on improving their English language skills. The passage was rough but it was all forgotten when we spotted the skyscrapers of New York City and then the Statue of Liberty.

The ship stopped near Brooklyn for the night. I was full of excitement and awe as I stood outside on the deck watching the traffic on the Shore Drive. I was completely fascinated by my view of this new and wondrous city. When night came the large neon signs lit up. There was one which baffled me completely, it read: "Seven Up." It was green in color and blinked on and off; I couldn't figure it out. What could this be - a number Seven and it's up? When I came ashore the next day I finally figured it out and, I might add, it was then, and still is, my favorite soft drink.

In the morning, the immigration officials got on board and the processing began. We received a document in lieu of a passport as our personal identification, and a handshake along with these words: "Welcome to your new country. Here is twenty dollars to get you started, good luck." The Fayerman family now had eighty dollars in their possession, and with these funds and a couple of suitcases apiece, we stepped on American soil, or, 12th Avenue, to be exact.

It was a beautiful spring day - rather warmer than we were used to - the time was 10:30 in the morning. We were met at the dock by my father's cousin, Harry Froot, and his wife, who were living in New York City. I asked if they could direct me to the Travelers Aid office. Instead, they took us there in a taxi. Travelers Aid provided us with free accommodations for three days in a hotel on Broadway. That night, we were invited to dinner at cousin Harry's. Thus, my first meal in America took place at a comfortable apartment in the Bronx. After dinner, we walked out in the street to look at our new world. I had my first milk shake, which was very good. I even remember it was a strawberry shake, a rather large one. I loved it! Just as I loved my first impressions of and experiences in this wonderful country that I already knew was going to be the home of my dreams.

The New Beginning

The family, consisting of my father, mother, Uncle Simon and me, gathered in the hotel room on Broadway for our first breakfast in America. We bought a few rolls and four bananas which we washed down with large cups of coffee. It all tasted so good!! After we finished eating we deliberated what we should do next. My father, who always presided at family consultations, suggested the obvious - that we start looking for jobs. We asked cousin Harry for directions on finding employment and he suggested the local employment office. My Uncle Simon and I were the first "displaced persons" to apply for work at the Manhattan downtown State Employment Office. I landed a job in two days as did my Uncle Simon. Father went to the Polish Consulate where his prison buddy had been made the Consul General in New York.

Thus, one week after landing in New York City, we all reported to our respective places of employment. My father got a cushy job at the Polish Delegation to the United Nations. My uncle landed an engineering job at a plant in Long Island and I went to work at a tool and die shop in lower Manhattan on Lafayette Street.

The day we received our first paycheck was filled with joy and pride. We could hardly believe our good luck. We were all paid in U.S. dollars and the total sum, to us, was a fortune. Although my father received the highest salary, I was very happy being able to contribute towards the family's upkeep. Not wanting to take advantage of the wonderful assistance we received from Travelers Aid in housing us in hotels, I started diligently looking for an apartment. It was very difficult at that time to find housing any place in the U.S. The G.I.s were returning from the war, getting married and looking for places to live. Fortunately, I found an apartment in the Bronx. It was a five-story walk-up at 1044 Avenue St. John. Whenever I gave my new address as Avenue St. John, people would correct me saying in America you say St. John Avenue. However, as fate would have it, this was the only avenue in the Bronx which was named Avenue St. John. I had a most difficult time convincing everyone that I was saying it correctly. Such were the tribulations of a newcomer to a foreign land.

Spring and summer went by. In the early fall the family gathered once again to discuss our future in the new country. My father was adamant on our pursuing the goal of re-establishing the family business in America. He said, "This is the best time to start a new company in the USA." Using these words as our motto, we started to explore how we could get into manufacturing again. We felt we had the know-how and could succeed given an opportunity.

All of our friends thought we were crazy! Their arguments were: you just arrived in this country; you are not completely fluent in the language spoken here; you don't know anything about the way companies are run in the United States; and above all, you don't have enough money to start a new company. It's impossible, they insisted; you will never succeed. My father's ears were deaf to all of these arguments. He directed me to quit my job and seriously start to look for a company to acquire. He felt the $6,000 the family had deposited in the bank was enough funds to get us started.

The funds came from the earnings of my father and me while we were employed by the Red Cross and United Nations respectively. As civilians working for the American forces, we were paid in script money, which was worthless in the USA. Thus, on the advice of my fiscal officer, we had refused our salaries and had them credited instead to our accounts. When we arrived in the United States, we claimed our pays and were paid approximately $3,000 each. These were the funds we intended to use for the purchase of our new venture.

I began my search by carefully studying the New York Times. I contacted several companies offering their businesses for sale. I visited many of them but for various reasons did not like what I saw. Most were not in the metal forming business, which was the field we knew best. Then one day I noticed an ad: BALDWIN TOOL AND DIE COMPANY for sale in Newark, New Jersey. I took the Hudson Tubes to Newark and met the owner, Mr. Ernst Horn.

He was a German immigrant with a very heavy German accent. The shop he owned was located in the heart of downtown Newark, at 5 Kirk Place, which was a narrow alley surrounded by factory buildings and bars. It was very close to the main railroad station. Not a very nice neighborhood to say the least, but I ignored all of that. To me it was ideal. The shop consisted of 3,000 square feet with a small office near the only entrance. The shop equipment consisted of four punch presses which ranged from two to twenty-five tons, several drill presses, work benches, and a selection of tool-making equipment of old vintage. There was no loading dock, and the trucks delivering and picking up goods had to stop in the middle of the alley, blocking traffic. Thus, all goods had to be unloaded and loaded by hand.

I started negotiations but thought Mr. Horn was asking too much money. To help me, I consequently included my father in the discussions. He spoke perfect German and got along very well with Mr. Horn, and the deal was struck. Our offer of $30,000 for the business was accepted. The terms agreed upon were a down payment of $5,000 in cash and the balance of the purchase price paid in installments.

We opened for business on January 2, 1946. The first and only employee we hired was an American Indian named Joe. We soon discovered that he frequented the nearby bars; however, while he was sober he did a good day's work. Fortunately, we inherited some contract stamping business which Mr. Horn had initiated years earlier. We were thus busy from the start. Our crew consisted of my Uncle Simon, myself, and Joe, our employee. My father worked part time. He kept his job at the Polish Delegation and came to the office to do the bookkeeping and billing after putting in a full day in New York. Late each evening, all three of us traveled back to the Bronx where my mother waited for us with a good dinner. I remember falling asleep on the subway train, tired after a long day at the shop. However, everyone in the family was enthusiastic and full of hope for our new beginning.

In the spring I found a nice rental house in West Orange, New Jersey. We shared the house with the owner, a retired high school teacher. She occupied the upper floor and we lived on the first and second floors. I bought a very old car from Mr. Horn and now, after working all day in the shop, we only had a short, twenty minute ride home.

Our business picked up as we landed several orders for punch press tooling as well as several contracts for stamping and assembly. We were not fussy; we took whatever job came our way so that we were able to keep the payment schedule with Mr. Horn. On weekends, the entire family made excursions to various parts of New Jersey and New York to explore our new country. We were pleased with our lives but longed for a product line of our own, which we could market directly to the stores rather than working as subcontractors to other manufacturers. We were trying to determine what we should make. Our expertise was in manufacturing bolts and nuts but the cost in machinery and inventory would be entirely beyond our meager means. Consequently we turned to the other side line we made in Poland; namely, door and window hardware and tools. Our business in Poland resembled (on a smaller scale) the conventional hardware manufacturers in the USA at that time - companies like Stanley Works, Reading Hardware, and Sargent and Company.

I began to frequent hardware stores considering available product lines. I was awed by such giants as Stanley and Sargent. The scope of their line was entirely beyond my comprehension, but I thought maybe we could pick out a few good sellers from their lines and thus start our own range of hardware. I purchased a good array of products as samples to consider for our own production, but could not decide which ones to attempt.

Then one day, a friendly customer brought in a letter box plate and suggested we consider it as our product. It was entirely stamped out of brass strip, a perfect item for our present equipment. I wrapped it in clean tissue paper and went to a local jobber to see if I could get an order. I introduced myself as a representative of Baldwin Manufacturing and offered a new product which we were producing. The buyer was surprised as (of course) he had never heard of us, but was sufficiently impressed by the item and the price to give me an order for one gross. I visited three other wholesalers on that day and everyone asked me if we could deliver. I assured them that this was a new product with us but we were in the process of making it. Everyone then gave me an order.

I returned to the shop elated and proudly showed the new orders. We were convinced then that it was a salable product. The next day, we started making tools for the very first item of our own hardware line. We worked feverishly on the set of tooling required for the letter box plates. In the meantime, we ordered the appropriate strip brass in coils from the local warehouse. As the stamping of the new product started, I looked into polishing equipment since the plates had to be highly polished and lacquered. We found a used polishing lathe which we installed near the window due to a lack of dust exhaustion equipment. I knew how to polish because in Poland we manufactured a line of trowels which had to be ground with fine abrasive.

The final step in the production of the letter slot was lacquering. We bought an inexpensive spray booth, a spray gun and a few gallons of lacquer. I found a man who agreed to come after work and spray our letter box plates with clear lacquer. I just needed one lesson with him, and the following day I was polishing and spraying all the items we made for the orders on hand. Packing and boxing were left to my mother. We ordered a supply of labels and as was customary, packed three of the letter box plates to a box. Now we had to decide how we were going to number our very first product. I suggested number 301 since the product consisted of three parts and it was the first item of our own manufacture. This product is still in our catalog as of this writing. It traditionally remains the first item one will find when opening our general catalog and it has been renumbered 0001 to conform with our new computerized numbering system.

As soon as an order was completed, I delivered it personally to each and every one of our new customers and then went immediately to the purchasing office and asked for another order. I was rebuked for taking so long in filling the orders, but I assured the buyers that this being our new product we had production problems which were now fully overcome. I assured them that we had stock on hand and could deliver at once. Well, they believed me and each customer gave me another order. We were on our way!

I began calling on all wholesalers and jobbers in the greater New York metropolitan area. It was easy to get orders at that time. Many existing manufacturers had not yet converted to full civilian production and were still filling their defense order obligations. It was very fortunate for us that we started the business near a large city, as this location provided us with a market close to our operation. I continued to personally deliver all of our products in Newark and vicinity, but we began shipping by truck or parcel post elsewhere.

My father would bill all shipments the same day and mail the invoices the same evening, hoping to receive payment quickly as we were obviously very short of cash. We drew no salary and were fully supported by my father's income. Thus, our overhead was kept very low.

While making my calls on our customers, I inquired what was in short supply and what they needed most. As a result of this information, little by little, we added new items - all stamped out of steel since brass was too expensive for our meager resources. Most of the first additions were barrel bolts, square bolts and small specialty items for the building construction trade. The first real boost to our business came when we started making replacement door knobs, the two-piece variety with a square slide on shank. This was a good item which we produced in large quantities and shipped to other states. Next came glass door knobs and finally brass replacement knobs with threaded shanks and set screws. Now we were offering a larger variety of products and printed our first catalog sheet. It was a legal size sheet printed on both sides, which I would leave with my customers. Soon we were able to print our second catalog which consisted of two 8" x 11" pages. We were getting reorders, some coming from as far as Boston, Massachusetts. Our pride grew day by day and so did our appetite for more products.

A welcome break occurred in the spring of 1949. During one of my visits to Whitlock Company, one of the largest locksmith suppliers, I was shown a bronze cast chain door fastener. I was told it was in great demand because the major supplier, Slaymaker Lock Company, of Lancaster, Pennsylvania was slow with deliveries. I bought a sample and took it back to the shop. The price Whitlock was paying was $1.80 each, which, in my estimation, was a lot of money. Although the product didn't fit our manufacturing capability, I hated to turn it down because of the good price it would fetch. We ordered the castings from a local foundry, bought the chain from a local jobber and began production. I numbered the item 485 and thought it would be a great money maker.

Several months later, I was laboriously grinding the bronze castings while thinking that it was a very difficult item to produce. At the noon break, I stopped the grinding and went to wash my hands. I was covered to my elbows in bronze dust which had colored my shirt green. As I was munching on my sandwich, I mentioned to my Uncle Simon that there must be a better way to make this product. He was sitting on the opposite side of the table and started to draw a design very similar to our No. 485. However, it was made of extruded brass with open ends on both sides, which was a distinct departure from the conventional shape. I spent the afternoon making a handmade sample of the new design out of a piece of yellow brass. I completed it that same evening, polished it to a bright finish, lacquered it and was ready the following morning to show it to Mr. Stern, the buyer at Whitlock who had introduced me to this product.

Quick calculations in the morning revealed that we could sell it for $1.00 per piece and still make a good profit. I decided on the way to New York to set the price at eighty cents each to make sure Mr. Stern would be interested and give me an order. Well, he was delighted and gave me an order for two gross. I realized my mistake in pricing and offered the same item at $1.00 each to my next customer. He gave me an order for four gross. The next customer paid $1.20 and by the time I returned to Newark that evening, I was getting $1.60 for them. We numbered our new chain door fastener 440.

We had an item! We ordered the extrusions and started tooling. Within six weeks I delivered the first batch. Our customers loved them. We couldn't make them fast enough and sold them to all at $1.85 each. This was the first item on which we made money and we were able to print a neat, folder-type catalog.

It was now time to expand our sales beyond the United States. I had been eyeing the Canadian market with great interest. During the summer, I drove to Montreal and called on prospective buyers and, using my knowledge of the French language to my advantage, I was able to write a lot of business.

Happy about my accomplishments, I decided to reward myself with a weekend in the Laurentian Mountains, which were a relatively short drive from Montreal. This decision resulted in an important personal change in my life. Not knowing anything about available accommodations, I drove until the road ended. There was a sign near the road advertising Mount Tremblant Lodge. I followed the directions and checked in at the resort about noon. There was a lake nearby and I thought it would be nice to take a dip. On the way to the lake, I met two ladies - one middle-aged and the other about my age. I asked them if I was taking the correct path to the lake. The older lady offered to show me the way since they too were going for a swim. I tried to engage the younger woman in conversation with very little success. However, this young woman eventually became my wife, mother of my children (twins - a boy and a girl), lifelong companion and my right hand in running Baldwin. Although she was active in practically every aspect of the business, she had the greatest influence in the selection of designs in hardware trim and eventually gift items.

With the addition of the new business I secured during my trip, we were now shipping coast to coast as well as to Canada and were on our way to success.

Eventually we made several designs of the same chain door fastener and, because we were now buying in large quantities, were able to buy directly from the brass mills. This put us in good standing with our suppliers who kept suggesting other brass products. They put us in touch with Accurate Brass Company, a custom brass forger. To show us what they could do, their salesman brought samples of the brass door knockers they were making for a gift manufacturer, Asia Brass.

The year was 1951. We were planning to expand our operation and I was looking for a better plant and location. I found a building in an industrial development in Hillside, New Jersey and we moved the plant in the winter of 1952. It was a modern facility in which we installed a proper polishing department and exhaust system. We bought a large lacquer booth and our number of employees reached 35 men and women. To keep the polishing department going, I needed more items made of brass. This was also the year that my Uncle Simon got married and left our association. My father and I bought him out. We were joined in the meantime by John, another brother of my father's. He had emigrated to the United States and lived with his wife Nella in Newark. There were three of us now. My father quit his job at the

Polish Delegation and worked full time at Baldwin. I ran the manufacturing operation, and my Uncle John was our salesman.

The business flourished as we continued to add more and more brass items. Our main source of supply of forgings was Accurate Brass. We were now offering a full array of door knockers and one forged brass letter box plate. Our major competitor was Ives Company of New Haven, Connecticut. I zeroed in on their line of products and within a period of three to four years, we became the alternate source of brass hardware products. Still, we needed more business. Ives was well entrenched and I couldn't dislodge their hold on the market. I decided to approach other large hardware manufacturers, like Corbin, Russwin, Sargent, and Yale, and offer to make the miscellaneous lines for them, freeing them to pursue the lock business, their major product line. It worked. We became a major supplier of door stops, bolts and door knockers to all the manufacturers I pursued. Unfortunately, the profit margin left for us was small and despite modernization, we were not making a lot of money. However, in retrospect, we were gaining invaluable experience in how to efficiently make these products in large quantities.

My Uncle John began to get huge orders for hundreds of door knockers from gift wholesalers. This was quite a difference from the orders for several dozen we were receiving from our hardware customers. Intrigued by this new source of business, I decided to accompany my uncle on his visits to the gift wholesalers to see what else they were selling in brass. I found their showrooms were displaying large amounts of decorative items (including candlesticks) at a very good price, mainly imported from Japan, England and India.

I realized that for me to make inroads on this market I must have an independent source of supply. Accurate Brass's prices began to escalate and our profit began to shrink. Remembering that before the war we had connections in England, I wrote to several companies asking if they did brass forgings. One company, McKechnie Brass, in Birmingham, England, sent a representative, Maurice Davis, (the son-in-law of the owner) to talk to us. He quickly realized that there was a tremendous opportunity in selling brass forgings to the markets in the United States. He proposed a joint venture. It sounded interesting and I flew to Birmingham for discussions, but I was not impressed with McKechnie's forging facility. It was a large operation and I felt their size and management style would not be a good fit for us. Mr. Davis came back to the United States for another round of talks. He suggested we try to discuss a joint operation with Ewarts, Ltd., also of Birmingham, England. Such a partnership would be beneficial for McKechnie as well as they were a major supplier of raw materials to Ewarts. After an exchange of letters, I was sufficiently interested in the possibilities and I eventually flew back to Birmingham. This time, I liked what I saw. Ewarts was a substantial company engaged mainly in custom brass forging. They had a large machine shop but their polishing operation was primitive. Most important to me, however, was the fact that they had extensive experience in operating screw type friction forging presses, exactly the type we had used in Poland.

Ewarts' management was very much interested in my proposal and we formed a new company under the name of Ewarts-Baldwin Forging Co., Inc., with Ewarts owning 51% of the shares. Their investment consisted of supplying five forging presses and ten turret lathes, plus training of our personnel in the operation of the forges.

The foundation of the new joint venture coincided with our move to Reading, Pennsylvania. The year was 1956. In the prior years, after receiving notices of various hardware equipment auctions and plant closings in Reading, I had made several trips to that city looking for a likely place to build our first permanent installation. I visited one plant, Penn Hardware Co., prior to the auction. I didn't find anything of interest to us, but I was very much impressed with the city and the workers I met, one of whom, John Hospidor, who had thirty-five years of experience in the hardware industry, wrote me a letter offering his services. He was willing to relocate in order to continue working in the business. I could not use him at that time, but I did hire him after our move to Reading. He became head foreman of our punch press department and stayed with me until his passing.

I talked to a number of city administration officials, the Reading Chamber of Commerce and Sidney Kline, Sr., President of Berks County Trust Company. I was very pleased with my reception; however, I was expecting a favorable tax treatment for our company as an inducement to move to Reading. None was forthcoming. Consequently, I started to look elsewhere for a possible re-location site. I went to Lancaster where two hardware companies had been located for many years. I also visited Bethlehem but they were not interested due to the major influence of the Bethlehem Steel Company. I went to York, Wilkes-Barre and finally Scranton. At the latter city, I was most welcome and promised a free, custom built plant as an inducement to move there, but I did not believe the labor attitude of the displaced miners would he favorable to our operation. After due consideration, we decided to move to Reading, but my Uncle John felt he didn't want to invest in the expansion project and opted to sell his share to my father and me.

With the cooperation of the Chamber of Commerce and the bank, as well as the efforts of Sidney Knoblauch, a local industrial realtor, we were able to buy seven acres of land at 841 Wyomissing Boulevard, in the city of Reading. The price we paid was unbelievably low. This was due to the fact that a great deal of pressure was exerted on the seller in order to accommodate us. It was one of many favors the concerned leading citizens of Berks County bestowed upon us - proof of the business community's leadership and foresight.

While the plant was being built, I commuted every weekend between Hillside, New Jersey and Reading. I was anxious to witness the progress of the construction. We entrusted the construction to R.S. Noonan Engineer-ing Company of York, Pennsylvania. They lived up to the agreed upon con-struction costs and delivered the plant on time in the spring of 1956. The move went flawlessly; however, none of the New Jersey employees came with us. While riggers erected the machinery in our new plant, I interviewed ap-plicants at the State Employment Office in downtown Reading. We hired approximately twenty plant and office employees to start up the operation. Within the month we had a total of thirty-five Berks County craftspeople on our payroll.

Preparations were made to install the forging presses and commence pro-duction. Ewarts Ltd. sent one of their forging experts, William Hudson, to train our press operators. They also sent several sets of forging dies for door knockers to enable us to start production promptly.

The main plant, which we still call Building No. 1, contained the entire hardware manufacturing operation. The receiving dock doubled as a shipping dock, next to which we had the shipping tables, and then the packing tables and stock room. Behind the stock room was the punch press department. Against the west wall was the polishing department and by the office door stood a vapor degreaser. Against the north wall was the tool room and a separate enclosure was built to house the lacquer booth. Finally, there was a wash room against the east wall and an adjacent cafeteria table completed the nucleus of the plant. Although it appeared very small, it was a very efficient operation which allowed us to plant our roots in the fertile environment of Berks County. My full attention was now directed to the operation of the plant. My father took care of the office with the help of my wife Marjorie. We did very well and prospered quickly.

The turning point came in late 1957 when I hired a pattern maker for our tool room by the name of Elwood Shaeffer. He turned out to be not an ordinary patternmaker, but a mechanical genius. Elwood spent his apprenticeship at the Reading Hardware plant. When the plant closed, he went to Penn Hardware Company as a tool room machinist, and when that plant ultimately closed he went to Earl Hardware Manufacturing as tool room foreman. I had just hired a friend of his who told him about Baldwin. Elwood realized the climate at his new place of employment was unstable and he came to Baldwin for an interview. I offered him a job as tool and die maker with a very modest salary as we were not able to afford high-priced tool makers. He was noncommittal and promised to let me know his decision. I nearly forgot about him when he called me one day saying he would accept the position since he wanted to stay in hardware manufacturing. Although Elwood was an accomplished pattern maker, he readily adapted to our forging processes because of his experience with hot metals. I sincerely attribute a large measure of Baldwin's growth and success to Elwood's intelligence and talent.

The first job I gave him was to build a simple tool to pierce holes in .050" thick push plates. Elwood couldn't believe his eyes. He asked me if I really intended to make door push plates out of such thin metal. I assured him this was a new trend and that we could sell many of them. Reluctantly, Elwood agreed to make the tool. In the course of our operation, we sold millions of push plates in varying sizes, some as thin as .038".

The following year, Ewarts sent their tool room foreman, Mr. Walter Barrington, to our plant to make sure we got off to the right start in making forging tools, which are a crucial part of the forging business. I began traveling to the eastern and midwestern manufacturing centers of the United States, drumming up business for our newly formed Ewarts-Baldwin Forgings Co. We landed many good orders, mainly in the fluid handling valve business. I stayed away from the decorative trade, wanting to save those products exclusively for Baldwin.

Several years passed and we were beginning to outgrow our facility. We decided to expand our polishing department and erect a new tool room building. We moved all buffing and degreasing to the new building leaving coloring and satin finish in the original location. We also installed our first automatic buffing machine. I had great difficulty convincing the traditional hand polishers to try the automatic machine. They all told me one could not get a good finish on an automated machine, that the hand touch was needed in order to get a high luster. Finally, I picked the oldest of my hand polishers and convinced him to try the new automatic because it would be physically easier on him. Reluctantly he agreed. His name was Arnold Glass, a first class polisher with forty years of experience. I assisted him in getting started until he finally told me to leave him alone. At noon break, I returned to see Mr. Glass. He was all smiles; his face was beaming. "This is fantastic," he said, "I would never have believed it but our knobs are coming off of this automatic better and faster than I could do them by hand!" Mr. Glass completed his working days on the door knob automatic and became my instructor on the new additional automatics we were constantly installing.

The new polishing building was then, as it is now, devoted to hand grinding, polishing and degreasing. An explosion-proof enclosure was built to house a water-filtered spray booth. A separate building was erected on the northeastern corner of the property to house an enlarged and modernized tool room. It had benches along the west wall and tool making machinery throughout the remainder of the area. Along the forging press room was a rack for tool steel and a metal cutting saw.

In the year 1962, we decided on another substantial expansion which would double our capacity. An office complex was built on a level above the plant. We occupied the ground floor only, leaving the second story for eventual future expansion. Consideration was given to a third level but this did not materialize, to my great chagrin. I dreamed about having my office on the top floor overlooking the city of Reading. This, however, never came to pass.

The new plant addition (which we numbered Building 6) housed an expanded turret lathes department and a new receiving bay. The forging trim presses were moved out of the punch press room to the west wall of the new building. The first in-plant office partition was erected at the northwest corner of the new facility, and any unoccupied floor space was used for the ever-expanding inventory.

Due to the growth of our product lines, all of our catalog sections were expanded as well - especially the contract hardware division sections "e" and "d." We were constantly bidding on various large construction projects, landing a good portion of our bids. We soon became a very important factor in the contract hardware business. However, as the years passed, I became disenchanted with this very competitive business. We were simply getting too big and couldn't effectively compete in the construction field. Many smaller competitors sprang up all over the country and we began losing orders to them.

We dissolved the association with Ewarts in England in 1963. We bought out their 51% interest in Ewarts-Baldwin and merged it with Baldwin Hardware. We stopped soliciting custom forgings business, concentrating on building our own line of forged products for the builders' hardware trade. We quickly became the innovator of brass forgings in the American Builders' Hardware Trade. Soon, we were the leader, out-distancing all of our competitors by a large margin.

Sadly, on June 7, 1964, my father and co-founder of Baldwin passed away. I had to abandon my daily supervision of the plant operation and assume the presidency of the company. Fortunately, I was ably assisted by my talented wife Marjorie. She managed the office while I looked after the general operation. However, every day from the beginning of the first shift to about 11:00 a.m. I continued to make my rounds of all departments in the plant.

Year upon year, we continued to add more items to our line. My goal was to make us the most complete supplier of hardware in the USA. In every item of our manufacture we were more diversified than any other supplier of the same product, and our gift line continued to expand. We were now exhibiting at numerous shows throughout the country, gaining more national recognition.

We continued to add more sections to our general catalog, expanding the existing sections, "a" through "e," the mainstay of our line. Contract hardware made the largest contribution to our yearly sales. This helped introduce us to many architects and strengthened our position with contract hardware houses throughout the country.

The most significant turning point for Baldwin occurred in 1968. While in Williamsburg, Virginia, searching for new items in the gift line, I came across rim locks. I was astounded to discover that a gift shop in historic Williamsburg was offering a range of rim locks and H and L hinges made of cast brass. What irony, I thought, here was a gift line manufacturer making locks and we, a hardware producer, were making candlesticks and such. Further investigation revealed that the locks were not made by Virginia Metalcrafters, the authorized manufacturer of Williamsburg reproductions, but by a prison lock maker in Peoria, Illinois.

I bought one mid-size lock and took it apart at the plant. The case and some internal parts were made of brass castings. The locks were poorly made and the functions were most basic. We deliberated with Elwood Shaeffer for a long time on how to make the rim locks in our shop. We had no problem with the internal parts, but the outer case could not be forged. After considering various means of production without success, we shelved the project for nearly a year. Then, in February of 1969, Elwood and I went to the Philadelphia Welding Show. There we saw a new stud welding machine capable of welding steel to brass, which was the missing link in our plan of production. We formed the outer case of the lock out of 1/8" thick brass sheet and stud welded all the necessary parts for the operation of the lock. We introduced three sizes in several functions incorporating lock cylinders for a convenient and secure method of installation. Our price was half that of our competitors and our locks were considerably better than the cast brass types available at that time. We were very successful with the rim locks and soon got all of the limited, available market. Many architects, intrigued by our locks, began to specify them on their projects and our reputation soared.

Now we added sections "f" and "g" to our general catalog - section "f" contained lock trim and section "g" the new rim locks. We expanded the lock line to many sizes and functions. A prominent architect in Ohio decided to specify our colonial brass rim locks on a large expansion project at the University of Ohio. He asked us, however, to incorporate the modern commercial functions used in public buildings. We complied. He was delighted and specified them on the entire project. Unfortunately, the total cost of hardware became too prohibitive, even on this very prestigious edifice. The architect was very disappointed but suggested making mortise locks instead. Little did he know that this was my ultimate dream. We asked him if he could promise us the job if we were able to produce the locks conforming to rigid building code standards. He assured us the job would be ours as he still planned to use a number of rim locks on the job and he wanted all the trim to match; consequently, the entire building project had to come from one manufacturer.

We enthusiastically went to work. This, we thought, would be an opportunity of a lifetime. The size of the University project was large enough to allow us to amortize the cost of the tooling, and, thus, enter the mortise lock business. The rest is history. Incredibly, every year after year, we added approximately one hundred new products to our line.

In 1973, we introduced narrow backset, lever handle locks with the largest assortment of locksets in the industry. In the Baldwin tradition, we offered a large selection of designs from traditional to modern. Sections "h" and "l" followed, while we managed to expand all other sections of our catalog and the gift line. The growth continued and still does to this date, making Baldwin a most dynamic company in the builders' hardware industry. Our products are superior to all of the competitors because we have never lost the drive to produce the finest quality products in the world. We are looking confidently into the future, creating new products on a seemingly never ending basis.

Retrospection

I often muse with gratitude about my fate which allowed me to survive the concentration camps. Although I believe good luck was a factor, there was an overwhelming inner drive to survive which propelled me through many difficulties and helped me negotiate dangerous incidents during my incarceration.

In these *Memoirs*, I purposely omitted recounting many horror scenes which I witnessed in the concentration camps. Time has helped somewhat to heal these old wounds. I felt it was not germane to my story to describe specific atrocities which would serve no purpose but to upset me and the reader. It is best to remember the good in people. Without doubt, I would not have survived the camps had it not been for the help I received from many individuals during those darkest days of my life. I am forever grateful to them for their kindness, often extended at great personal risk.

Most thankful am I, however, for the fact that I survived the horrors of World War II with a positive attitude towards life and people. I am happy, glad to be alive, proud to be an American, and fully intend to continue living every day to the fullest.

CPSIA information can be obtained at www.ICGtesting.com
Printed in the USA
BVOW000500120713

325729BV00004B/19/P

9 780983 331070